GOD'S G

Dedicated to my Mom, Carol Anglin.

A true example of Self-Sacrifice.

Thank You for giving up of yourself so
that I might benefit. I pray that I can
sacrifice myself, as you did for me, for
my wife and children.

GOD'S GAME!!!

BY: BRANDON ANGLIN

INTRODUCTION

I grew up playing baseball. I was always one of those kids that enjoyed playing all sports, but there was something about baseball that I loved. Maybe it was the challenge of it. I always found it more difficult than football or basketball. There were a lot of mental aspects to the game that made it difficult. Any sport where you

only get 4-5 chances to succeed in a game is difficult.
Think about it. Most hitters get three at bats per game.
Lots of times position players only get 2-3 chances per game
to make plays. So, 4-5 times per game to be great, or 4-5
times to fail. Plus if you make an error or strike out, you
have to wait a long time to make up for it. That's tough! I
don't think I ever really liked the pressure of it. But as
much as I didn't like the pressure, I loved the challenge of it.
I never walked away from football or basketball games
feeling drained mentally, but baseball can do that to you.
There were many times when everything inside of me
wanted to quit on baseball. I could write an entire book on
struggles I had as a player and times I wanted to give up.
But there was always something about this game that drew
me back in. I really can't explain it. Why didn't I stick
with basketball or football? I had a lot more success in
high school playing those two sports. Maybe it wasn't my
choice. Maybe sticking with baseball was all part of a
bigger plan that the Lord Almighty had from the very
beginning. Although there were many struggles in this
game, the blessings far outweigh those tough times.

Along with baseball being challenging, it can also be kind of slow. Except for diehard fans, most people would call it boring!! I think most baseball players, if they were honest, would tell you that they don't really enjoy watching an entire game. I always have a lot of respect for those "old timers" that just show up to high school or college games to just watch. They don't know any players. They have no connection with either team. They just love watching the game. My grandfather Hoyt Langford was like that. He could cut an Atlanta Braves game on and watch every pitch from start to finish. On the other side of that spectrum would be my wife. Although, she might not ever admit it, my wife does not enjoy watching baseball! But, for the past 17 years she has been supportive of my passion for this game. She has watched me play in high school and college. And for the past 11 years she has always been faithful to attend games and support me as a coach. For that I will be eternally grateful.

Over the years I have thought a lot about baseball. I had the opportunity to pitch for the University of Georgia. I was never very successful, and the mental part of the game always gave me struggles. When I first started coaching, I realized there were a lot of aspects to the game I did not understand. Truth be told, I never really studied it. As I said earlier, baseball has so many facets that require you to "think." As a coach, I have loved that challenge. I have taken those mental difficulties I had as a player and used them to motivate me as a coach.

Outside of loving baseball, I also have a passion for the Lord. In 2010, my spiritual life changed for the better. It started me on an amazing journey in which God started opening doors that never had been opened before. I had the opportunity to meet a very godly woman who has guided me every step of the way. Although the last two years have been times of Spiritual Growth, they have also been times of difficulty. During this time, I have started to see things differently and God has allowed me to have a different perspective on many things, like Baseball!!!

That leads me to the idea of this book. In the summer of 2012, I was lying in the bed one night and started to think about all the connections between baseball and the Christian Walk. I started to jot down some ideas and then kind of got stuck in my thinking. I laid it down and never did anything with it until December of 2012. The ideas suddenly started to get better and better. God started to open up my thinking again. It's amazing how God tells us that "My ways are higher than your ways and my thoughts than your thoughts." I want to make it clear that I am not a pastor, priest, counselor, or any other type of theologian. I am simply a Believer who teaches Special Education and coach's baseball in high school. I don't have any special credentials that would draw you to this book. I am a high school coach that loves baseball and Jesus Christ.

Baseball and Christianity. What in the world, right? That is what I first thought when God first laid it on my heart. While playing Little League Baseball for Bill Ormsby and Luther Wilkes on the Giants back in Little League, I never thought I would be looking at baseball in this fashion. My main goal is that through this book, you will grow to understand the beauty of both. Hopefully you will grow in your walk with Christ. Maybe there are aspects of Christianity that you are not sure about that get answered here. And maybe people, like my wife, will start to appreciate baseball. Maybe, just maybe!

There are 10 chapters in this book. Each chapter begins with a baseball discussion and then connects it to an aspect of Christianity. At the end of each chapter I have included some discussion questions (7 EACH CHAPTER, 7 INNINGS!!!) that I hope will allow you to apply that particular concept to your life. Maybe you and others will read through this book and discuss it together. Some of the discussion questions will require the use of a Bible. Writing this book has been a blessing to me and I hope and pray it blesses your life as well!

TABLE OF CONTENTS

6. LULL OF THE GAME (THE DISTANT TIMES)

7. WINS (BLESSINGS)

8. 9 PLAYERS (SPIRITUAL FRUITS AND GIFTS)

9. GEAR AND UNIFORMS (SPIRITUAL WARFARE)

10. A ROUND OF INFIELD/OUTFIELD (GETTING PREPARED FOR OUR DAILY WALK)

CHAPTER 1: THREE STRIKES AND THREE OUTS (THE TRINITY)

In baseball the concept of 3 is vitally important. From a defensive standpoint being able to get 3 strikes or 3 outs will greatly determine your success. There have been times in my coaching career when getting those 3 was not difficult. I have been blessed to coach a lot of very talented pitchers that could dominate innings pretty easily. I have always preached to pitchers that the key to success is getting outs. We don't necessarily care how "pretty" it is. We just want those 3 outs. I have heard many pitching coaches across the country talk about the same concept. "Just get outs," many of them will say.

Getting those crucial outs has a lot to do with the pitcher. The pitcher controls the game. He has the ball in his hand more than anyone else and controls the pace and flow of innings. There is a lot of pressure on him. The spotlight constantly shines. Maybe that is why I always struggled as a pitcher. I don't really like the spotlight, and I struggle handling very stressful situations. Even today, I struggle sometimes with the pressure of being a father, husband, teacher, coach, believer, FCA leader, school leader, Sunday school leader, and so on and so on!! There are many aspects of my life that I have learned, and am constantly learning to give to the Lord. God can handle the pressure!!!

Now, I would be lying if I said that getting those 3 strikes or outs has always been easy as a coach. There have been many times I sat in the dugout calling pitches just praying that the opponent would just hit it hard right at someone on our defense to get us out of an inning. There is nothing more miserable than sitting there calling pitches, watching your pitcher get hit, or walk guys, or watching the defense make errors. I enjoy chewing sunflower seeds. And it is during those innings when I chew the most seeds. Nervous habit I guess. Could be worse right?? Watching long innings while on defense is a helpless feeling and I have been there many times in my coaching career. But to be honest, although they are miserable at the time, those bad innings don't stick with you. They are easy to forget. I guess God just has a way of taking those painful times in our life and helping us to wash them away.

I remember two summers ago having a conversation with one of my freshman pitchers. He is a really talented LHP that has the ability of being really special. But as a young pitcher he struggled to finish innings. There were so many times I saw him get the first two hitters out but then give up runs in the same inning. I ended up talking with him after one of his outings about keeping his mentality throughout the inning. I told him that every inning he got the first two hitters out, I wanted him to try and strike out the next guy. My hope in telling him that was to keep his aggressive mentality. As a pitcher, there is nothing great about 2. 2 strikes or 2 outs don't make you a successful pitcher.

While the concept of 3 is crucial to the game of baseball, our understanding of the Trinity is even more important in our Spiritual Walk. To be honest, I didn't always understand the Trinity. My Spiritual Walk began with God, transitioned to Jesus Christ, and then flowed to the Holy Spirit. Those are the "3"!!! As a Christian our understanding and application of the Trinity will determine our success as believers. It sounds so strange to describe the Trinity in this manner, almost as if it is something that is not tangible or real, but I think we have to have this understanding of which each is in order to grow in our relationship. Hopefully you will see how real the Lord is throughout this book. The Trinity is three facets of God; The Trinity is not three separate Gods, There is only one God. I know this can sound a little crazy. Hopefully the rest of this chapter will explain it. The power of 3! Father, Son, and Holy Spirit.

15 "If you love me, keep my commands. 16 And I will ask the Father, and he will give you another advocate to help you and be with you forever— 17 the Spirit of truth. The world cannot accept him, because it neither sees him nor

knows him. But you know him, for he lives with you and will be[a] in you. [18] I will not leave you as orphans; I will come to you." (John 14: 15-18)   Here Jesus clearly discusses the idea that there is this concept of "3".   While speaking of Himself, He mentions a Father, and a Spirit: This is the Trinity.   Another key verse that the Bible gives us is Mathew 28:16-20.   These verses are most commonly known as the Great Commission: "Then the eleven disciples went to Galilee, to the mountain where Jesus had told them to go. [17] When they saw him, they worshiped him; but some doubted. [18] Then Jesus came to them and said, "All authority in heaven and on earth has been given to me. [19] Therefore go and make disciples of all nations, baptizing them in the name of the Father and of the Son and of the Holy Spirit, [20] and teaching them to obey everything I have commanded you. And surely I am with you always, to the very end of the age."   Once again, Jesus makes reference to the Father, Son, and Holy Spirit.

How does all this fit together and what is the importance of the Trinity?   In order to grow in our Christian Walk, we need to have an understanding of the importance of the Trinity. The truth is our salvation and our life journeys depend on this understanding. Salvation depends on knowing that we are born as sinners and have a separation from God. We have no opportunity at Heaven without Jesus. The key here is that we need to understand how much God abhors sin. He detests sin, He cannot be a part of sin, and therefore we have no opportunity to be with Him because of our sin. Fortunate for us, God sent his Son Jesus to earth to save us from our sins and allow us to enter into eternity with God.

Grace and Mercy. I was in college when I truly started to understand these terms. I still remember to this day sitting in the baseball locker room having a Bible Study with Ray Lawrence. Ray was talking that night about Grace and Mercy. Definitely terms that I had heard before, but for some reason they had not become attached to my comprehension until that night. I finally got it!! I saw just how amazing those concepts are!! I am still thankful to Ray for the many hours he invested in me at GA. We had a lot of 'coffee shop" talks and he helped to hold me accountable during a very distracting time in my life.

Mercy is not getting what we should get. In this case, we deserve Hell, but through Jesus we get Heaven. Grace is receiving something we don't deserve. In this case God gives us forgiveness that we don't deserve. John 3:16 says: "For God so loved the world that He gave His one and only begotten son, so that whoever believes in Him shall not perish but have everlasting life." God loves us so much He allowed His son to come to earth, be punished, crucified, and even worse took our sin upon himself. The beauty of it all is that God sent Jesus to save us while we were still sinners (Romans 3:23). How amazing is that? I have thought about this many times. I am blessed to have two beautiful daughters, and I can promise you that I would die for them tomorrow if I had to. Not even a tough decision. But what about those sinners out there? What about those rapists, adulterers, thieves, murderers? Could I die for them? If I was asked to die for one of them so that they would have an "opportunity" to be saved, would I do it? I don't think so!! Luckily for me I don't have to even consider that question. Because **we all** have a Savior available to us through Jesus Christ.

I like to think in simple terms. So far here is what we have:

1. Problem------We are born separated from God because of our sin!!!!

2. Solution-----We can spend eternity with God if we accept the free gift of salvation that He gives us through His son Jesus Christ!!!!

One thing I had to learn in my life is that my salvation has nothing to do with me. It is all about Jesus. At a young age I found it difficult to see myself as a sinner, because as humans we weigh sin. We see sins like stealing and killing as worse than lying or gossiping. It was important for me as a believer to learn that God despises all sin. Are some sins worse than others? Yes! Some sin has greater earthly impacts than others. Of course, murder will have a greater earthly impact than will gossip. But, from God's perspective all sin is detestable!!!! Hebrews 1:9 says that God loves

19

righteousness and hates lawlessness.   And Psalm 5:5 says that God hates all evildoers.   Once again, we are guilty as charged!   All of us have sinned, are sinning, and will sin again.   Without the sacrifice of Jesus we are destined to a life separated from God. The truth is you and I am no different from the worse of criminals.   The only difference is that I have accepted the Grace of God and the Gift of Jesus.

So, where in the world does the Holy Spirit fit into the picture??   I think the Holy Spirit is probably the most difficult concept for the average Christian to grasp.   I love Francis Chan.   I had the opportunity of reading his book *Forgotten God*.   My understanding and faith in the Holy Spirit grew from reading that book.   The Holy Spirit is an integral part of the Trinity, yet many Christians fail to see the significance of Him in their daily walk. Sounds weird right? Referring to the Holy Spirit as a person??   It is easy for me to see God and Jesus as physical beings, but throughout my life the Holy

Spirit has many times been this "thing" that is hard to grasp. Do we really need the Holy Spirit? The answer is YES!! In John 14: 25-26 Jesus says, "25 "All this I have spoken while still with you. 26 But the Advocate, the Holy Spirit, whom the Father will send in my name, will teach you all things and will remind you of everything I have said to you." A couple of important notes to make here:

1. Jesus says He is leaving and that God will send the Holy Spirit to counsel us.

2. The Holy Spirit is the Counselor

3. The Holy Spirit is referred to as He.

Man that is powerful!! As you can see, the Holy Spirit is real. Jesus says that He will leave and while He is gone the Holy Spirit will be here to counsel us. Jesus goes on in to say in John 16 that He must leave so that the Counselor can come. I remember when I was growing up in Holly Springs United Methodist Church we would cite the Apostles Creed every Sunday. The end of the Creed says "I believe in the Holy Spirit." That's easy, and for much of my life, that is exactly what I did. I believed in the Holy Spirit. Yet the New Testament of the Bible says that the Holy Spirit is much, much more than just something to believe in. Why would Jesus make such a point of discussing the Holy Spirit to the Disciples? The Holy Spirit was alive and powerful in the lives of the Apostles and is alive and powerful in our lives today. We just have to take advantage of Him. In the book of Acts the Apostles were filled with the Holy Spirit. When this happened they were changed!!! People saw something different about them. Many thought they were drunk, but it was only 9:00 in the morning! I guess it's possible to be drunk that early. I went to the University of Georgia and have actually witnessed drunken college students this early, but I would venture to say that this was not the case with the Apostles.   The book of Acts is a fascinating read.   After Pentecost and the filling of the Holy Spirit, these believers go on to grow the Church exponentially.   They also perform miracles and heal many people just as Jesus did.

Not only does the Holy Spirit work through believers in our everyday lives, but He also is an intercessor for us.   Romans 8:26 says that "[26] In the same way, the Spirit helps us in our weakness. We do not know what we ought to pray for, but the Spirit himself intercedes for us through wordless groans."   Other Bible versions says that the Spirit "intercedes" for us.   What does that mean?   When someone intercedes for us they act or interpose on our behalf because of a difficult circumstance that we are in.   I love Galatians 4:6 that says "[6] Because you are his sons, God sent the Spirit of his Son into our hearts, the Spirit who calls out, *"Abba,*[c] Father."   We need to pay special attention to the fact that Paul says here that the Spirit "calls out." He could have used other terms or words, but he

23

obviously felt the need to stress to us that the Holy Spirit does not go quietly to the Lord for us. He calls our cries out to God on our behalf. Isn't that reassuring? Especially for those of you who might feel as if you have never had anyone in your corner. Maybe you feel that there has never been anyone that protected you. Well, believe me when I say that you do!!

The power of 3. In baseball we have to be able to get 3 strikes or 3 outs in innings to be successful. It's not always easy, but it sure is fun when you are good at doing it. As a believer we must understand that there are 3 aspects of God. The Father, the Son, and the Holy Spirit. Our salvation and our daily walk depend on our understanding of this Trinity. Let's get those 3! Our baseball victories will be determined by it, but more importantly, our salvation and spiritual walk will.

PRAYER:

God you are beyond my comprehension. I thank you for who you are. Thank you for creating me, saving me, and guiding me every day. Thank you Jesus for your sacrifice on the cross. Thank you Holy Spirit for working in me each and every day to connect me with the Father and guide me towards righteousness. I pray that my life will bring you Glory and Honor! AMEN.

LET'S PLAY: DISCUSSION OF

CHAPTER 1

1. The Trinity is _____ aspects of God.

   _____, Son, and _____

   _____.

2. All 3 aspects of the Trinity are part of the 1 God, but

   they are all different.   How so??

3. Is there any part of the Trinity that you feel

   inadequate in?   (remember for me it was God,

   Jesus, and then the Holy Spirit)

4. Read back over John 14:15-18.   How does this verse give us a clear picture of the Trinity?

5. Do you have knowledge of the Trinity or a relationship?   What is the difference?

6.   If you had a relationship with the Trinity, what would be different about your life?

7. Are we missing out on the Fullness of God (Ephesians 3:19) if we don't grow in our relationship of all Father, Son, and Holy Spirit?

CHAPTER 2:   ERRORS (SIN)

Is there anything worse to watch than "bad baseball"?   As I said earlier, a lot of people think baseball is boring.   We baseball fans don't believe that, but, coaches and fans will tell you that watching a game full of "bad baseball" is awful.   Probably the largest contributing factor to "bad baseball" are errors.   Errors!   Man that word will make any coach cringe.   A team that makes lots of errors has no shot at winning big games.   Most of our successful teams at Loganville High School have been really solid defensively.   I have been blessed to coach with others who are great teachers of the game.   Fortunately for us, we have every facet of the game covered by a coach.   As I said earlier, we have talented players, but no doubt these guys who I coach with are crucial in the development and success of our teams defensively.

But, here is the deal, teams are going to make errors.   We are human.   Guys will screw up physically or lose focus mentally and that will lead to errors. Unfortunately many of those errors will lead us to lose ballgames. I have been on the losing end of many games as a player and coach. A great number of those losses were because of guys making errors. It is hard to win games committing errors. Truth is, defense can go unnoticed many times. Nobody gets excited about a routine groundball going to second and the fielder making an easy throw to first to get the batter out. The only time defense is noticed is when it stinks! I remember in high school that Coach Dubose, my basketball coach, had a sign in our locker room that said "Offense wins games, but defense wins championships." That saying always stuck with me. It applies to every sport. The better defensive team has a greater chance of winning. I once read that in Major League baseball, the team with fewer errors in playoff series won 70% of those series. Not a coincidence!

I will take a team that has pitchers throwing strikes and the defense making plays over a great offensive team. When I was in the 8th grade I was a manager for our high school basketball team in Jefferson, GA. I loved being

29

a part of that team. They were really good. I still have a plaque from that team and I remember that it said they averaged 96 points per game. If you don't know, that is a ton for high school basketball. That team was ranked #1 in the State pretty much all year. But just as good as they were at scoring they were equally as bad on defense. They got beat early that year in the State Tournament. It had everything to do with defense. I don't care what sport it is, the better you are defensively the greater chance you have to win. Defense never has bad nights. Bad defense can destroy your team. A team that makes errors will not win big games.

Just as errors are part of the game of baseball, and an ugly part at that, sin is a part of every one of our lives. We are all sinful human beings. As my friend "Chappy" says, "we are all jacked up." Romans 3:10 says "There is no one righteous, not even one." Just like players, we all make mistakes in life, we all sin, and we all screw up. I am a sinner. I sinned before I knew Christ. I sinned after I knew Christ. I will continue to sin while I walk on this earth. I really struggled with this as a young believer. I thought once you got saved you should remove sin from your life. That led me down a path of living a life drenched with guilt. Every time I sinned, I got mad, and down on myself, and felt very distant from God. Now, there is some good in that. We should feel convicted when we sin. We shouldn't like it, but by no means should we walk around feeling guilty about our sin.

For an **unbeliever**, sin keeps him from ever being able to see God. For a **believer** sin keeps us from growing in our walk with Christ. Once we accept Christ as Savior, we become a part of God's team. In other words, we are forever sealed. 2 Corinthians 1:22 says, "He set his seal of ownership on us, and put his Spirit in our hearts as a deposit, guaranteeing what is to come." I love that word "seal." It's almost like we have been branded. Once we give our life to Christ, we are now locked into His Team, the greatest team we will ever be a part of!! I remember being in college, once again I was not very good, having to worry every year if UGA would ask me to leave, if UGA would take my scholarship away and cut me. You see, I was not some great high school pitcher that came in with lots of accolades.   Truth told, I signed a scholarship with UGA

because of one workout at a showcase at the University of

Auburn.   I was a tall, left handed pitcher that had a good

arm.   There was a lot of potential in me.   I was a dream for

a coach.   But, I had no idea what I was doing.   I didn't

pitch much in high school.   I had never heard of a

changeup and didn't even know what a 4 seam fastball was.

I honestly was not ready to pitch in college.   But, I signed

anyway and went off to UGA.   My first year there I

redshirted.   It was pretty much a wasted year and I didn't

get any better.   It seemed like I then spent the next 4 years

playing catch up.   I felt that I went into every year trying to

remove those past labels I had.   I feared I was that guy who

"never pitched in high school, came from a small school,

couldn't throw strikes, was redshirted." Those labels kept

me from ever being truly confident that I wouldn't at some

point be asked to leave the team.   It wasn't until my senior

year that I knew my place was "sealed" on that roster and in

that program.   I played with other guys who had the same

fear, and have now been in the game long enough to know

that many players at many different schools and levels

worry about that same thing. Thankfully, we never have to fear that with God's team. We cannot be kicked off. We will never be cut; regardless of our errors, regardless of our mistakes, regardless of our past, regardless of our failures, and regardless of our "labels." We have to hold on to this truth. There are times when our past experiences can impact our present view of God and God's Love. Once we have made the decision to become a part of God's team we have sealed ourselves eternally. That should bring us relief. We are now seen as Righteous, and God no longer sees "us" when He looks, but instead He now sees the righteousness of Jesus Christ. What a great TEAM!!

The point is that regardless of whether or not we are a believer, we still have to deal with our sin. I have known lots of Christians, and have even experienced myself, getting caught in a sin as a believer. For example, many Christian men struggle with pornography. You see sin is fun; it is great. If sin wasn't fun, we wouldn't do it. Even as a believer sin is something that we must fight every day. And we lose that battle much of the time. Satan is very good at what he does. The Bible says that he comes to steal, kill, and destroy.   And he will use everything at his

disposal to do that, but it's not all Satan's fault.   We have

to also accept much of the blame for our sin.   Let's be

honest, sin is fun!   Nonbelievers like to look at the sin of

believers and use that as "evidence" that they are fake.

"They are hypocrites", they like to say.   Really?   Where in

the Bible does it say that once we become believers sin will

disappear?   That is a misconception of the world.

Hebrews 11 is a great reference to explain this point.   This

chapter is many times referred to as "Heroes of Faith."   In

other words, these guys are pretty good.   I would love it if

someone called me a Hero of Faith.   Hebrews 11 lists all

these mighty men and women of faith in the Bible.

Heroes!!   Men and women like Abraham, Noah, Sarah,

Moses, David, Samson, Isaac, and Rahab.   Every one of

them did great works for the Lord.   Every one of them were

the definition of a believer.   Yet, every one of them lived

lives that many times fell short of the Glory of God.   You

see, becoming a believer does not mean you will never

struggle again.   Sin will still be tempting and we will still

fall short many times.   But, God's grace will still be there.

All of these men and women did great things for God in spite of their sin.   Even if you have fallen recently as a believer, don't allow that to be a reason you don't seek to do what God has called you to do.   If David would have committed adultery and then just gave up as a Believer he might not have ever been the Godly father he was to Solomon.   We are told in the Bible that he instructed Solomon to walk with God and that was **after** the affair with Bathsheba.   God never gives up on us.   He is never happy with our sin, but He also doesn't want us to sit around and feel guilty about our shortcomings.   We should never give up on ourselves.   When we sin, then we repent, and after we repent then we seek to do good for the Lord!!

The fact that we will always continue to sin does not give us a free pass to just live however we desire.   The Bible says in 2 Timothy 2:22 that we should pursue righteousness.   Ephesians 5:1 says that we should become imitators of Christ.   Why?   Why does it matter how we live once we are saved?   Many Christians struggle with these questions.   I have often heard my pastor talk about many Church going Christians who seek to get their "fire insurance" and then live however they want. The concept is easy to understand, but the application is sometimes very difficult. As believers we are saved, by the Grace of God, and we should strive to live lives that are pleasing to God. Will we fail? Yes. And when we do, we confess, and get back up and continue to "pursue righteousness." The beauty of righteousness is that we will never be able to obtain it. There will always be aspects of our lives that fall short of God's standards and His idea of Righteousness. If we are to have a substantial impact for God here on earth, it is crucial that we live lives that are pleasing to Him.

Errors can ruin a game, just as sin can ruin our lives. As a player I have made many errors in ballgames during my playing days. As a man I have committed many sins during my life. As a coach, I will have to watch many more ballgames that are full of errors. As a Believer, I will continue to commit sins and fall short of the Glory of God. The good news for my players is that I will continue to pat them on the back and encourage them to keep working when they make errors. And as a Christian man, God will continue to pat me on the back and encourage me to keep

working when I sin.   Praise God!

PRAYER

Dear Lord, please forgive me for the sinful life that I live.

Forgive that I constantly fall short of your glory and

standards.   Thank you for your grace and mercy.   Thank

you for Jesus.   Thank you Jesus that you endured the

cross so that I might experience the Glory of Heaven.

Strengthen me as a believer to resist Satan and face the

temptations of this world.   And when I do fall short, I pray

that you will help me to get back on my feet and continue to

pursue righteousness.   AMEN.

LET'S PLAY: DISCUSSION OF CHAPTER 2

1. What is sin?

2. Have you ever truly asked God to forgive you of sin in your life? If not, why? (THERE IS NO BETTER TIME THAN RIGHT NOW)

3. Even if you have confessed and you are a believer in, do you still struggle with sin today? Is there a difference between "sinning" and "living in sin?"

4. What are some practical ways that you can work to overcome sin? (Ex: Accountability partners)

5. What is the difference in confessing sin and repenting of sin?

6. When was the last time you repented of a specific sin?

7. Do you allow your struggle with a sin to make you feel guilty and make you useless for the Body of Christ?

CHAPTER 3:   4 BALLS (THE GOSPELS)

I honestly don't think there is much worse in baseball than watching hitters walk.   Ball 4!!   That is a painful thing to hear an umpire say.   I wish I could say that I was good in this area as a pitcher during my playing days. But I was AWFUL!!   I walked and walked and walked and walked (I think you get the point) hitters!!   I bet coaches stayed so frustrated with me.   I now know that because as a pitching coach, I hate when my guys walk hitters.   I stay on them constantly about throwing strikes and forcing contact.   4 Balls will get you beat.   There are so many studies and so much data that proves that if you walk hitters as a pitcher you will struggle to win games.   The odds are weighed heavily against you.   I could easily spend a little time in this chapter naming past pitchers I have coached that could not throw strikes.   I could give their stats and you would be able to see how much walks hurt them throughout their career. But instead, I think I will focus on those guys who avoided 4 Balls. Those guys that figured out how to throw strikes consistently. Some of the best guys that come to my mind are: Garrett Ford (LHP 2012), Kenny Anderson (LHP 2011), Landon Hayes (RHP 2010), Clay Garner (LHP 2010), Kyle Doehrman (LHP 2005), and Wade West (RHP 2004). I hate to leave off some other guys that I have had that were really successful pitchers, but these guys could really throw strikes. All of them knew how to "pound the zone." There were very few times that we went into a game worried that they were not going to throw strikes. All pitchers have off days, but for the most part, all of these guys were going to avoid walking hitters. Their stats showed it and most of them went on to successful college careers. Have we had other guys that struggled to throw strikes but were successful? Of course!! There is an exception to every rule, right? I think of two pitchers right now that are good exceptions to this rule: Christian Miller (LHP 2012) and Casey Shiver (RHP 2010). Both of these guys struggled at times to stay in the zone.   They walked more guys than we would have liked, but both had really good stuff and were able to get out of jams because of that.   They both were eventually drafted and have enjoyed good careers.

This chapter is interesting!   I titled it 4 BALLS.   I just spent the first page discussing how much I hated Walks, how I hate when pitchers throw 4 Balls and walk hitters.   So how in the world am I going to connect "4 Balls" to the Gospels?   The Gospels are the FOUR most significant books of the New Testament.   They are written by Matthew, Mark, Luke, and John.   Each of the four Gospels tell stories of the life of Jesus.   They each go through the early life of Jesus and end up with His death and Resurrection.   All FOUR Gospels have many verses of Jesus' words.   The very first book I ever read in the Bible was when I was about 14 years old.   I sat down and just started reading the book of Matthew.   I kept seeing all this red typing and I wasn't real sure what it meant.   I now know, and so should you, that the red typing in the New Testament of the Bible are the words of Jesus, the spoken words of Jesus.   Paul, James, and John are all great but they fail in comparison to the teachings of Jesus. As a believer in Jesus Christ, the most significant books in all of the Bible are the Gospels. The term Gospel derives from the Greek word meaning "good message." We have already discussed what Jesus came to do for us and what He still does for us today. If you have never read any of the Gospels, I invite you to do so today. Put this book down and dig into the Word of God. Discover who Jesus was through Matthew, Mark, Luke and John. Ephesians 5:1 says that we should walk as Christ walked. Or in other words, we should imitate Jesus. How can we do this if we don't read about His life and His teachings? The Gospels give us a clear picture of who Jesus was and allow us to "pursue righteousness" as we are called to do.

From a historical perspective, The Gospels are some of the strongest, most validated writings in ancient times. Historical writings of Julius Caesar, Roman Emperors, and other popular Religious leaders fail in comparison to the writings of Matthew, Mark, Luke and John. One of the measuring sticks that historians use to validate past writings is the gap between a person's life and when it was actually put on paper. The Gospels were written no more than 30-50 years after Jesus was on earth. With all of the social media and technology at our expense today, that number sounds really long. But, for ancient writings, that number is actually really good. Matthew and John are mentioned as being of the 12 Apostles, so they would have been very close to Jesus. Mark and Luke were not Apostles, but they lived during that time and were close to men like Peter and Paul. What am I trying to say? The Gospels give us a really accurate picture of who Jesus was, what He did, and what He taught. It is written by men that lived during that time period and in that same area. Very few ancient biographies can say what the Gospels say about Jesus.

So, as 4 Balls are bad, the Gospels are good. As a pitcher, throwing 4 balls consistently will make it difficult to succeed, but in contrast, as a Believer it is essential to read and study the 4 Gospels on a consistent basis. There is no better way to have a relationship with Jesus, than to learn who He was, what He taught, and what He desires!! I pray that everyone who reads this book will follow it up with a study of Matthew, Mark, Luke, and John. I pray that the Gospels will encourage, and at the same time, challenge each and everyone one of you as they do me. Many times believers will spend time reading books written by great authors like Max Lucado (I love his books), David Platt, or Francis Chan, and neglect the greatest writings we have at our disposal: THE BIBLE. I have read all three of those guys mentioned above and feel confident in saying that they would all encourage us to spend time in the Gospels before reading their books. There is nothing wrong with outside readings, but remember nothing should take the place of God's Word. Study the Gospels!! Allow them to deepen your understanding and relationship with our Lord and Savior, Jesus Christ!

PRAYER

God, thank you for your Word. Thank you for sending your Son to forgive us of our sins. Thank you for providing the Good News. Thank you for the Good Message of Jesus. May we be encouraged and challenged as we study the life and teachings of Your Son!! AMEN.

LET'S PLAY: DISCUSSION OF

CHAPTER 3

1. The Gospels are _____ books in the Bible.

   They are Matthew, _____, _____

   and John.

2. How are they similar and how are they different?

3. The word Gospel means "Good News." What is

   good about these books in the Bible?

4. Why are reading the Gospels significant for a

believer?

5. Do you take the Words of Jesus directly and attempt to apply them to your life? Give an Example

6. Much of the Gospels feature Jesus teaching in parables. What are parables?

7. Read Matthew 22:36-40. What does Jesus say is the greatest commandment?

CHAPTER 4:   LOSSES (STORMS)

Baseball can be a bear!   As a player and a coach I have been part of some bad teams, teams that just couldn't win and teams that almost found ways to lose.   That's how we classify good and bad teams right?   The ones who win are good and the ones who lose are bad.   Think back to all of your days as a player or coach, and I am sure you remember some of those teams.   Some of those teams might have been full of very good players.   I remember experiencing that as a coach.   In 2004, we had one of the best teams in the state.   Or better yet, we had one of the most talented teams in the state.   One problem.   We didn't win.   I don't know what it was.   Nobody does.   We, the coaches, all looked for solutions.   We tried to figure out what the problem was.   I remember there was one time during the season when Coach Segars decided to just cancel practice for a couple of days and have the guys show up for the next game.   I loved it.   A couple of days off during the middle of the season.   I got caught up on some sleep.   But that didn't work either.   They just couldn't win.   Plain and simple.

Losing stinks.   I don't know about you, but I am an extremely competitive guy.   I don't like to lose.   I have been in arguments, confrontations, and a few fights over sports.   I even think some of them were over sports video games.   For years now, a group of coaches at my high school have met at 5:30 AM on Tuesdays and Thursdays. You would think at that time, there wouldn't be a lot of arguing or competitive spirit.   You would be sadly mistaken!!   We go at it.   I have had to apologize to some guys afterwards for losing my temper during the game and acting in a way I was not proud of.   That's sad!   But, like I said, I am competitive, and if you have played or coached sports, odds are you are too.

Baseball is also the one sport where a less talented team can really have a great chance at winning.   You take a low talented baseball team, and put a great pitcher and catcher combination with them, and they can beat anyone. One or two guys can really make a big difference in baseball.   That's another thing I love about the game.

There are a lot of games we go into nervous, because we know the team we are about to play is not great, but they have that one good pitcher. He can beat you! That's frustrating. You know you practice more than they do. You know you teach more. You know you spend more time in the weight room. Frustrating! But, that is one more beautiful aspect of this game.

As a pitching coach, I have to also deal with injuries. I have been fortunate as a coach to not have many guys get hurt, but unfortunately it has happened. I see these injuries as losses. In fact, I would rather lose every game during the year than to lose a guy to an arm injury. I take arm injuries very hard. I do everything possible to make sure my pitchers do not get injured. Just as sometimes you can do everything possible to prepare your team for success and still lose, you can do everything possible to protect your pitchers and they still get injured. In 2010, we lost our closer the last week of the season to Tommy John surgery. I spent weeks after the season researching the internet trying to figure out where I went wrong. What could I have done to protect him? Was it my fault that he tore his UCL? It was tough. This game can drive you nuts. To be honest, I got angry. Why did we get an injury? "I work my butt off trying to protect our pitchers." I'm pretty sure I even stated a couple of times: "It's not fair!!"

Doesn't life work like that sometimes? Don't we sometimes look around at other people and ask why do they get all this good stuff? Why is their life so good? I am a good person. I do right. I give to others. I shouldn't have to go through these "losses." In baseball we call these tough times losses, and in life we call these tough times storms. The storms of life. Never fun. Always painful. And sometimes more than we think we can bear.

We've all encountered storms in our life. I know I've had my fair share. Where do I even begin? Parents divorced when I was 9. Dad remarried another woman that wreaked havoc in my family's life for years. Dad had virtually nothing to do with me in high school and college. Mom, who I lived with, battled alcohol for many years, we never had a ton of money in comparison to some of my

51

friends. Mom had to eventually work two jobs. I signed a scholarship to play baseball at the University of Georgia, only to sit on the bench and never really find success while there. I went through a tough couple of years of identity theft, with constant phone calls by creditors that really stressed me out. My first daughter was diagnosed with severe acid reflux that would cause her to stop breathing at times. She had to wear a heart monitor for her first six months. I was diagnosed with an anxiety disorder at the age of 30, which creates some ups and downs in my life still today. And so on and so on. Enough complaining, huh? Some of you will read this paragraph and say "that's it, let me tell you about my life." Others will read this paragraph and say, "Wow, it sounds like you have had it really tough. I can't imagine." Well, here's the truth. That's life! Storms will come and storms will go. We will all experience them throughout our life. Some are tougher than others. Jesus even warned us about difficult times in John 16:33 when He says: 33 "I have told you these things, so that in me you may have peace. In this world you will have trouble. But take heart! I have overcome the world."."

In baseball, we can learn a lot from losses. As a coach, we can really take advantage of the lessons that losses bring our way. After losses players are more likely to focus on their weaknesses and ways that they can improve. I read a quote one time by Austin O'Malley that said "if you learn from a loss you have not lost." Obviously there is a play on words here, but man is it true. Any type of loss can offer us lessons that will benefit us. Some of the best conversations I have had with players have been after they failed in a game. Maybe they went 0-4 or pitched awful or made a lot of errors. It is at that point that you can get their attention. It is at that point that they are willing to listen and take a little coaching. It is at that point that lessons can be taught and learned.

Storms of life do the same for us. Sometimes it takes difficult times in our life for us to "wake up." Is this a hard concept to buy into? You better believe it. But if God's Word is true, then we must trust Paul when he said in Romans 8:28 "that in all things God works for the good of those who love him, who have been called according to his purpose." All things! Paul doesn't make a distinction between the good and the bad. He says that everything works together for our good. We must hold on to that truth when the storms of life sweep over us.

One of the most Godly women I have ever met is a great example of this. Mrs. Q. is a great Spanish teacher that I have been fortunate enough to work with for many years. She and I have only really known each other for about 3 years, even though we worked with each other for 8 years before that. Remember earlier in the introduction when I mentioned a "Godly woman" that helped lead me to a deeper relationship with the Lord? That was Mrs. Q! Her story goes as follows: She was a Christian for many years and eventually was "saved" while serving in the US Military. She attended church regularly and was good as far as she was concerned, but everything changed when she was diagnosed with Breast Cancer. During her time battling this awful disease, undergoing Chemotherapy and Radiation, she connected with the Lord like never before and was forever changed!! She says that she now realizes that she was far from God. She realized that it wasn't about church, or doing a devotional, or a Bible study from time to time, but it was all about a relationship. The "storm" changed her. God allowed her to undergo an awful experience for her benefit.

Is everyone like Mrs. Q? No. There are many believers and nonbelievers who go through difficult situations, get through them, but don't change. Mrs. Q could have easily stayed the same after defeating cancer, but she "woke up." A friend of mine told me once that we should never waste our suffering. Mrs. Q certainly did not. She allowed her "storm" to take her to another level with the Lord. What a challenge that is!

Can we see the storms of life as opportunities? What if the difficulties that we face in life all have a greater purpose? I will be the first to tell you that it's tough. Seeing difficulties, storms, and losses as opportunities to grow is not fun. I can think back to some tough situations that I have gone through and my first response was: WHY?? Why me? But here's the truth. Just like baseball teams rarely go undefeated in a season, we will rarely go a long period of time in life without storms hitting.

Even if you screw up and have the wrong attitude during one storm, God will offer you other chances.

Mrs. Q not only allowed her cancer to bring her closer to the Lord, but she now uses it to bless other people's lives. I have seen her go and speak Truth into many teachers and students lives at the school. Myself included. It is a multiplication effect.

1. Mrs. Q goes through a storm.

2. Storm is used to draw her closer to the Lord.

3. She eventually sees the storm as opportunity.

4. She uses storm to bless and teach others.

5. Those "others" then go and use their lessons to help others.

6. MULTIPLICATION!

I did an awful job of this for much of my life. I mentioned earlier some of the difficulties that I experienced throughout my life. I didn't understand that maybe God allowed me to go through them so that I could turn around and help others who experience something similar. As a coach for the past ten years I constantly see kids battle divorced homes, alcoholic or drug addicted parents, bullying, anxiety, depression, and so on and so on. What an opportunity I have to share. My mindset for many years was that God got me through those difficulties and now I was going to forget about them. What a bad misunderstanding of what God calls us to do with suffering. 2 Corinthians 1:3-4 says "3 Praise be to the God and Father of our Lord Jesus Christ, the Father of compassion and the God of all comfort, 4 who comforts us in all our troubles, so that we can comfort those in any trouble with the comfort we ourselves receive from God." What a cool message! We suffer, God provides, we then turn around and use our suffering to help others!!! I no longer try to hide my suffering. I try to be transparent because I realize that there are others that can benefit from my storms. I also have discovered that one way to get through a storm in our life is to bless someone else. Many times I think we make difficult situations worse because we focus so much on ourselves.   If we simply take our eyes off of ourselves and find ways to love and serve and care for other people, I promise the storm will get much easier.

All baseball teams will lose games and all people will go through storms in their life.   Do we enjoy losing?   No! Is it okay to not enjoy it?   Yes!   But, storms offer us the ability to grow.   Storms offer us the ability to learn.   They open our eyes.   They help us to analyze our weaknesses. And most importantly storms allow us to bless others.   I have seen players and teams grow the most when they go through losses.   I have experienced in my life that I have grown the most as a man, Christian, husband, and father when I go through storms.   DON'T WASTE YOUR SUFFERING!!

PRAYER:

Father, thank you for the storms that life has offered me.

That is difficult for me to say, but you tell me in your word

to be thankful for all things.   Please forgive me for my

attitude while I am in the middle of the storm.   Forgive me

for my lack of trust that You will carry me through the

storm.   May I use the storms of life to bless others.

AMEN.

LET'S PLAY: DISCUSSION OF CHAPTER 4

1. What has been the most difficult thing you have ever experienced in your life?

2. How did you get through that storm?

3. Is there a storm that you are going through right now in your life?

4. If you are not in the middle of a storm, did you learn from the past storm you went through?

5. Have you ever helped someone else to overcome a difficulty because of the lesson you learned from a past storm?

6. If you are not in the middle of a storm are you

    preparing yourself to handle a future storm?

7. Is there someone you know right now in your life

    that would benefit from you discussing a past

    difficulty that you have been through because they

    are going through something similar?

CHAPTER 5:   7 INNINGS (Biblical examples to follow)

High School baseball plays seven inning games.   I remember when I first started coaching, it felt like the games flew by.   I went from playing in a NCAA Regional at Georgia Tech on a Sunday and coaching on a Friday in a High School Summer game at Monroe High School.   Man things changed!!   One of the biggest things that stood out to me was how quick the game went by.   7 innings just didn't last long compared to 9.   You would think that 2 innings wouldn't make a big difference, but it really does.

A lot of things change in a 7 inning game compared to 9 innings.   The biggest difference lies in the pitching.   9 inning games normally require more arms to get through. Major League baseball even shows this today.   There are starters, long relievers, short relievers, set up men, and closers.   7 innings makes it a lot easier to manage your pitching.   You can get through a game with 2 arms about every time.   Many high school teams utilize two pitchers basically all year long. The 7 innings allows them to be able to do that. Back in 2008 we played Greenbrier High School from Augusta, GA in the Elite 8. They had a left handed pitcher named Nolan Belcher. He goes down as one of the best high school pitchers of all time in the State of Georgia and is currently pitching for the University of South Carolina. He was good and he only lost two games his entire high school career. Greenbrier had won two straight state titles and had a tradition of utilizing just two pitchers during their season and even into the playoffs. They had even used Belcher to throw game ones and then game threes in a best of three series!! 7 innings allows that. We had a deeper pitching staff and we knew it, but we also knew that we would probably have to beat Belcher 1 out of 2 times to win the series. We lost Game 1 to Belcher 7-0. But the good thing was Belcher had to throw all 7 innings. We threw a little sophomore lefty that was 80-81, but could really pitch named Clay Garner. That was our goal. Make Belcher throw a lot of pitches and all 7 innings. It was a 1-0 game into the fifth. It was the best 7-0 loss we have ever had. Long story short! We won game 2, even with Belcher coming back in to throw relief. He just wasn't the same guy he was in Game 1 and we beat him. When we beat him, they were done. We beat them Game 3 10-0 and that series really propelled us to go on and eventually win the 2008 State Championship. Point of the story? High School baseball is different because of the 7 innings. Teams have won titles with only two quality pitchers on the team. Amazing!!

I decided to label this chapter 7 innings. Most of the chapters in this book were easy to connect between Christianity and Baseball, but this one was difficult. God laid on my heart that it was necessary to have a chapter that is centered on people in the Bible that we can really learn from, so this chapter is 7 innings. We will take a look at 7 people in the Bible. 7 people that are just like us. They were humans that faced the ups and downs that life offers. Some of them had families. Some of them worked ordinary jobs. Some of them were major screw ups. Will important people get left out? Of course! But these seven have impacted me, and I believe they will do the same for you.

FIRST INNING: ABRAHAM

Every good baseball team needs a good starter. In baseball, the starting pitcher sets the tone for the team. A starting pitcher brings different components to the table than does a reliever. Normally starters have the ability to really pound the zone. In other words, they can throw strikes. They also can throw multiple pitches for strikes. Starters have to be able to turn lineups over. They must be able to face hitters multiple times. The better hitters will make adjustments and have a major advantage on the pitcher if the he cannot throw at least three pitches. Two pitch starters normally really struggle after a couple of innings. It's important to have that third pitch in your "back pocket." Starters lots of times are also a little more laid back then are relievers. Relievers many times are naturally a little more intense and "max effort." If you watch Major League baseball you see lots of starters who are laid back and smooth types of guys. Their delivery is normally less effort, and they have the ability to maintain velocity beyond 2-3 innings.

65

The starter that I chose in this chapter is Abraham. Why? Not really sure. I could give you some theological reasons connected to him being the first believer and establishing the First Covenant with God, but really I just decided to start with him. I don't want this chapter to make one Biblical leader seem any more significant than others. I think we learn from all of them in different ways.

Many of us remember as young kids singing the song about Abraham. "Father Abraham, had many sons, did many sons have Father Abraham. And I am one of them and so are you......" I still sing that song at times with my daughters. The song has a lot of biblical relevance. In Genesis 12, "The LORD had said to Abram, "Go from your country, your people and your father's household to the land I will show you.[2] "I will make you into a great nation, and I will bless you; I will make your name great, and you will be a blessing. [3] I will bless those who bless you, and whoever curses you I will curse; and all peoples on earth will be blessed through you."

From this point on Abraham will follow the direction and guidance of the Lord. It's important to note that

Abraham arose from an area that was mostly polytheistic. If you go back and study the history of this area, called Mesopotamia, polytheism was the main practice of the people. The idea behind polytheism is that there is more than 1 God. Originally most of the Gods of the Mesopotamia people centered on natural elements like sun, moon, rain, clouds, etc. So, establishing a relationship with One God was a strange concept to those people, and establishing a relationship with One God that you cannot see was even stranger of a concept. But Abraham trusted God. And because of his obedience he did eventually have a child named Isaac. Isaac will have a son named Jacob and the great nation that God promised Abraham had begun. Whew!!! What in the world is going on, right?? Here is the importance. Abraham trusted in God. He was an old man, his wife was old, and life was comfortable. But he trusted in God's calling that there were greater plans for his life. He had to take a step of faith. He didn't take this step of faith and one day later God's promise was fully revealed. But instead, Abraham took this step and had to trust in God over and over and over again. It took years for him to have his first child and in between that time and even afterwards life was difficult for him at times. His family and friends doubted God and the plans that Abraham believed He had for him.

As with all of the people in this chapter, there are lots of details that we could discuss with Abraham. There are lessons on top of lessons that are within the Scriptures, but I think it's important to look at one aspect of Abraham that we can learn from. Abraham had FAITH. What is faith? Faith is believing or trusting in something or someone. It is believing in something without proof of whether you are right or wrong. It is tough!! The Bible talks a lot about Faith. Most of the people that we are discussing in this chapter had faith. Many of them are mentioned in Hebrews 11 under the title of: "Heroes of Faith."

Abraham had FAITH. I can't stress that enough. As a believer, we must have faith. Without faith, there is no salvation. Without faith, there is no relationship with God. Without faith, there is no heaven. But faith is not easy to achieve. Faith is a day to day action. Imagine putting yourself into Abraham's shoes. Those of you who don't have a family will have a more difficult time than those of us who do. Abraham was living a good life. He was prosperous and successful in his job. He had a good family that supported him. Life seemed good. But Abraham believed that God was calling him to more. He believed that God had great plans for him and wanted him to go to a new land and father a great generation. The Bible says in Genesis 4, "so Abraham went." I'm sure there are some details that are not mentioned there. I'm sure he had to go and discuss it with his wife Sarah. I'm sure it took him a while to figure out how he would move his family, goods, animals, servants and so on. But all of those details are not important. We sometimes get caught up in the small details. The important thing is Abraham went!! He had the faith to step out there and go. Was he nervous? I'm sure. Did he question himself? I'm sure. Did he feel guilty when they got out there and life got tough for his family? I'm sure. But he remained faithful. Here is what we learn about faith from Abraham. First, faith requires us to take action. Second, faith is day to day.

We don't say that Abraham had faith because he left everything to follow God. We say that Abraham had faith because once he got out there and life got tough and people said he was crazy, he continued to stick to his faith. That's FAITH!

SECOND INNING: MOSES

If Abraham helps us to understand the importance of faith, I believe that Moses is a great example of helping us overcome the odds. Moses was a Hebrew that was born during a time period when it wasn't safe for Hebrew boys to be born in Egypt. Therefore his mother abandoned him and he was eventually found and raised by the Pharaoh's family. The Bible says that Moses one day went out to be among "his people." According to Exodus 2, Moses got angry when he saw an Egyptian beating a Hebrew and his anger turned to violence with him eventually murdering the Egyptian. Long story short: Moses got scared he would be caught and eventually ran off.

After running off Moses will settle down with a family, get married, and have a family. During this time

Moses has an encounter with the Lord. God calls out to Moses and tells him that He has chosen him to go and tell the Pharaoh that it is time for the Israelite people, God's people, to go.

It is at this point that we begin to learn immediately about Moses. His first response to God is to turn the job down. Moses says in Exodus 3:11 "Who am I that I should go to Pharaoh and bring the Israelites out of Egypt?" What an amazing beginning to this relationship between God and Moses. God appears to Moses and tells him (while speaking through a burning bush by the way) that he has been selected to go and get the people out of Egypt. Moses responds with "Really, you want me?" If you aren't laughing right now because you feel a connection with Moses, you might have the greatest self-esteem and confidence of any individual I have ever met. We all feel inadequate at times in our life. I don't care who you are. There are situations that we get into that cause us to be fearful and worried that we will not be able to get the job done. But, the beauty of this story is that God provided for Moses. He immediately rebuked Moses' fears when he began to make excuses. And guess what? God does the same for us. God desires for us to take our excuses and take our fears and take our worries and throw them out!! Just like with Moses and then Joshua after him, God provides. When we feel inadequate we must look at people like Moses and realize that he is not any different from us, yet God took care of him. Was it easy for Moses to get those Israelites out of Egypt? No!! It also took 10 plagues from God. I'm sure there were many times when Moses told God, "I told you I couldn't do it." But Moses stayed with it. He stuck with the promises that God made him Day 1. We must do the same. When you feel inadequate, realize that God is faithful and will provide what He has led you to do.

THIRD INNING: DANIEL

Can you imagine living during a time period when any given day could be the last day of your freedom, a day when there was no CNN or FOX NEWS? A day when opposing armies would attack without announcement other territories and destroy them. Invading armies would enter cities and burn them to the ground. They would kill many men. They would enslave many women and children. Sometimes they even made the men become eunuchs. Look that term up!! OUCH! This was the time when opposing armies would invade, take over, and force the conquered to change. Many times people's way of life would be forced to become drastically different. Religion was always a hot button topic. Think about religion. For many people their beliefs are the most significant aspect of their life. Imagine someone forcing you to stop your beliefs or to begin believing in another God or Gods. The thought of it will make many people cringe, but it happened. It happened thousands of years ago and it even still happens today.

There is an important story in the Old Testament about a man named Daniel that lived during a time period as this. His land had been taken over and his people forced to live under kings and peoples that were very different. Daniel lived under multiple kings. His story is written in the book of (strangely enough) Daniel. There are many lessons to be learned from this book, but the one that sticks with me is the commitment that Daniel makes to the Lord. While many people abandoned their faith during this time period because of the threat of persecution and death, Daniel stayed with his faith. He faced his fears and trusted that the Lord would protect him. Eventually, he is placed in a Lion's Den. The intent of putting him in there was for him to be killed by the lions, but he lives. Because of his faith, God protected him, And because of God's protection over him, the king and many others accepted the Lord.

What a good reminder of the opportunity that we have as believers. Life is tough; we are put in situations where we will be tempted to compromise our faith. We will be challenged to stick with our beliefs in the face of persecution or embarrassment. Luckily for us, we don't have to worry about someone killing us in America because we believe in God. But every day we come across people who are not believers. Every day we are put in situations where we are asked to trust in God. I know I fail at times!! There are times when I put more trust in myself or friends or "experts" than I do God. Daniel is a good reminder that

God asks for our trust and promises to never let us down.

FOURTH INNING: DAVID

Maybe out of all the people in the Old Testament, David gives us the most lessons.   There are so many aspects of his life that I could talk about and we could learn from.   He is talked a lot about in I and II Kings and I and II Chronicles.   He is also mentioned multiple times in the New Testament and is included in the Hebrews 11 Hall of Faith!   Many people know the stories of David and Goliath. Many people know that the book of Acts says that "he was a man after God's own heart."   Many people also know that David was a screw up.   David committed adultery with a woman named Bathsheba, got her pregnant, and then had her husband murdered.   WOW!!   Many people also know that he was a great fighter and powerful king that replaced King Saul and then fathered King Solomon.   Obviously, there are many things we could discuss with King David. If you have never done so, I invite you to study up on David. Lots of great lessons!

For this book, I've decided to look at one aspect of

each key Biblical character. I hope that we can learn something beneficial from all 7 Characters that I have chosen. So what should we look at with David? Patience! I remember when I was young that my mom told me I should never pray for patience. I was told that praying for patience would cause bad things to happen in my life. It scared me so much that I made sure I never used that word in prayer. She wasn't wrong in telling me that, just something that she had been told before. She was not serious about it, but I was too young to read that. But the truth is, patience is needed in our life. It is a required element of our walk with Christ. David is a good example of how life can sometimes operate on a different schedule than we would like. David was told at a young age by Samuel that he would one day become king of Israel. But it didn't happen overnight. It took many years before this prophecy would come true. Do you think David had days of doubt? Do you think there were times when David thought "this Samuel guy is crazy?" Have you ever felt that God was telling you something, but it just didn't happen when you thought it should? Have you ever been in a situation that you just wanted to hurry up and end, but it didn't? Learning patience is tough. David would eventually become king. He would become the greatest king that Israel ever had. We all deal with patience every day. Were there situations that you faced today that required patience? Is there something major going on in your life that is requiring you to be patient? If so, then follow the example of David.

FIFTH INNING: PETER

I always like to watch movies about the New Testament that has an actor playing Peter. They normally portray him as this loose cannon, a rough and rugged type of dude that loves Jesus, but really struggles with social skills. I recently watched a special that the History Channel put together called The Bible. It was a great series, and I really liked their portrayal of Peter, but as I watched, it also became clear to me that Jesus dearly loved Peter. Jesus saw something special in him.

Peter reminds me a lot of kids that I have coached. We have all had that kid that was constantly screwing up.

I think back to many teams that had that one kid, the one kid that was probably not worth the headaches he caused. He stayed in trouble on and off the field. People constantly questioned why he was allowed to continue being a part of the program. But like Peter, he had potential. He had gifts and talents that others did not. He had the potential to be a leader. There was a quality about him that was appealing. Man! Those kids hit a special spot in your heart!! There is just something about them that creates a deep desire within you to see their success. You go out of your way for them. You stick your neck out for them. And just like Peter does to Jesus, they question and abandon you at times. After all the stuff you have done for them, they desert you. If things aren't going well, they many times will jump ship. They will ask lots of questions, and most of them will be driven by selfishness. But in the end, most of these guys come through. They get the job done!! As did Peter.

In a short period of time Peter will go from the right hand man of Jesus to denying that he even knew Him. It would be easy to focus on Peter's denial of Jesus. But instead, one of the truly amazing aspects of Peter's story is how Jesus responds to him AFTER the denial. Following Jesus' death, Mary Magdalene and Mary mother of James went to anoint Jesus' dead body with oil, but when they went to find Him, they discovered that His body was gone. While there they had a conversation with an Angel. In Mark 16:7 the Angel tells them, "But go, tell his disciples **and Peter**, 'He is going ahead of you into Galilee. There you will see him, just as he told you.'" There obviously is a lot to the verse, but one of the cool aspects is that he says "and Peter." Why did the Angel need to stress to the two Mary's about Peter? I believe it's because the Lord wanted Peter to make sure he knew that Jesus still loved him and cared for him. Peter had done the unthinkable. He had denied Jesus. But Jesus was making it clear that He still had big plans for Peter.

What a lesson that we can learn here. We can learn from Peter's mistakes, and that even through the denial, Jesus still planned to use him. What if we viewed others mistakes with the mindset of Jesus? Just like that player that messes up more than he should, we continue to be persistent. We continue to look at the good in them. We continue to pray and hope that one day they will figure it out. Peter did! He becomes the leader of the Apostles and in the book of Acts leads the others in preaching and converting new believers. There is a plan for all of us!

SIXTH INNING: STEPHEN

Probably one of the most unknown Biblical figures is a man named Stephen. The book of Acts teaches us about him. He teaches us a great lesson about boldness. He is known as the first Christian Martyr. Someone who willingly dies to stand up for his beliefs. It would be easy to just glance at the story of Stephen and notice that he was stoned to death because of his faith, but there is more to the story. About three years ago Wayne Naugle, the Youth Pastor at First Baptist Church Loganville, discussed Stephen on a Wednesday night and said something that stood out to me.

There are passages throughout the Bible that mention Jesus "sitting at the right hand of God," It is a beautiful picture of the Father and Son spending Eternity together!! But in the book of Acts, while Stephen is being stoned to death, he has a different vision of Father and Son. Acts 7:55-56 says, "But Stephen, full of the Holy Spirit, looked up to heaven and saw the glory of God, and Jesus standing at the right hand of God. 56 "Look," he said, "I see heaven open and the Son of Man standing at the right hand of God." I hope you noticed something here. Stephen says that he saw Jesus standing at the right hand of God. So the question is why. Why was Jesus standing up beside God? This is the only time in the Bible that Jesus is mentioned standing beside God. I believe these verses make it clear how important Jesus takes our boldness. I can envision Jesus standing and clapping as Stephen is stoned to death, clapping because he is proud. Proud that Stephen stood up for his beliefs even in the face of death. I'm sure there are sermons and theological discussions out there that disagree with me, but Oh Well!!

We all need boldness in life. The Bible is clear when it comes to fear. We have to overcome fear as baseball players, friends, sons, husbands, fathers and definitely Believers in Christ. Stephen did!! He is a great example to follow when we feel fear overwhelm us.   There

have been many times in my life when I wasn't as bold as

Stephen.   To be honest, there have been many times when

I sat quietly when I knew God was calling me to take a

stand.   Why?   Because of fear!!   In all of those situations

(and there have been many) I allowed fear to overcome me.

How do we become more like Stephen?   We pray about it!!

God has made all of us individually and creatively.   Some

people are naturally more assertive and bold than others.

My five and two year old make that clear to me every day, for

they are completely different socially.   But, through the

Holy Spirit we can all stand up to fear.

SEVENTH INNING: PAUL

Paul is by far the most influential of all the early

believers.   He was ultimately responsible for writing the

majority of the New Testament.   If you study his writings in

the New Testament, you will also figure out quickly that he

plays a major role in the development of the early churches

across the ancient world.   Speaking in baseball terms,

Paul would be the Babe Ruth of Christianity.

As I have done with all of the previous figures from the Bible, I want to pursue one aspect of Paul. As I stated earlier, Paul played a major role in the development of the Christian Church. Looking at everything he did, Paul had every opportunity to be extremely arrogant, but from his writings, we find that he was a humble man. It seemed that Humility was one of his strengths. The Bible is very clear on Pride and Humility. There are multiple verses that make it clear to people that Pride can be dangerous. Proverbs 16:18 says, "Pride goes before destruction, a haughty spirit before a fall." Paul was adamant about Humility. And his writings show us that he had a humble spirit. One of my favorite verses in the Bible is Romans 9:3. In this verse Paul says, "[3] For I could wish that I myself were cursed and cut off from Christ for the sake of my people, those of my own race." What an awesome verse. It is clear that Paul understood the concept of Humility. The concept of flowing low. The concept of putting others ahead of yourself. The concept of desiring that the betterment of those around you is important. Paul also shows his humility by praying for other believers multiple times in the New Testament. Another awesome verse appears in Ephesians 3:14. In this verse Paul says, "For this reason I kneel before the Father." Paul will go on in verses 14-21 to offer up a prayer for the people living in a place called Ephesus. In this prayer, we can see the heart of Paul. We can see that Paul was willing to humble himself, to go to his knees before His father, for others!! He is not pleading to God here for himself, but for other people. That is Humility. We have to truly be willing to lay aside our concerns in order to do this. Question for you. How much of your prayer life is about YOU? How often are your prayers and thoughts for others? We will not pray and think about other people if we are full of pride. Only when we grow in Humility, like Paul, will we place others ahead of ourselves.

PRAYER

Father God, thank you so much for the Word of God.
Thank you for men and women of the Bible that lived lives
that we can learn from.   As life takes us through different
avenues, I pray that we might rely on the your Word and the
people in your Word to guide us.   Thank you for knowing
each and every one of us individually.   Amen.

LET'S PLAY: DISCUSSION OF CHAPTER 5

1.   Who is your role model today?   Is it an athlete or actor or some famous businessman?   What is it about their life that you most admire?

2.   Who in your life is a great example of someone who lives according to God's Standards??

3.   Out of the 7 Bible Figures discussed in this book, which one do you have the most in common with? Why?

4.   We talked about qualities that each of these Figures had.   Which quality would be the most challenging to you? (Faith, Overcoming Odds, Patience, Persistence in Beliefs, Forgiveness, Boldness, Humility)

5. If you are a believer, have you studied the people of the Bible to learn life lessons from them?

6. God did amazing things in many lives throughout the Bible. What about you? What has God done in your life?

7. Can you list some past events that you know God played a major role in?

Chapter 6: LULL OF THE GAME (THE DISTANT TIMES)

According to the dictionary, the term lull means to cause something to sleep or rest. If something lulls you to sleep, it must be extremely boring. In baseball, we refer to the middle innings as the "lull of the game." At the beginning of a ballgame, everyone is excited. At the end of the game, everyone is focused on trying to win. There is excitement in the beginning and there is excitement at the end. But many times the middle of the game is just kind of boring. I have witnessed many high school players lose focus during the middle of games. Even in some of the biggest games of the year, 16 year olds struggle to stay "locked in" for 7 innings.

We have lost some ballgames because of the "lull." One example that still stings me today was back in 2009. We were playing Starrs Mill high school in the Final Four. It was game 1 and we jumped up on them 5-0. We had a pitcher on the mound by the name of Clay Garner.

Remember him?   Little lefty that pitched Game 1 against Greenbrier.   He was one of the better pitchers that I have ever had the opportunity to coach.   And by far the most competitive pitcher that I have been around.   When we won our first State Title in 2008, we brought him in in the last inning with a 1 run lead, with 1 out, runners on 2nd and 3rd, and the middle of the order up.   He was only a Sophomore, but he came in and struck out both hitters to move us on to the State Title series.   He was a fighter!!   So, going back to 2009, we were up 5-0 going into the 5th inning (the LULL).   Clay was rolling along, but then the LULL hit. We walked a couple of guys, made an error or two, and then they got some hits going!!   Next thing you know we were down and ended up losing 7-6.   OUCH.   This was a huge game.   The field was packed with fans who were rowdy!! The dugout was rowdy!!   The players were rowdy!!   But, the LULL hit.   Sometimes you can feel the LULL coming on and can't really do much about it.

There are times when our Spiritual Walk can experience a LULL.   There can be time periods when we feel distant from God.   When our walk feels a little boring.

89

We might ask God questions during those times. Does God still hear me? Am I really saved? Why have I lost the fire that I once had for God?

The relationship between the two is amazing. In baseball it happens like this. Kids lose the emotion that they had in the beginning. Once the fire is gone, they start to lose focus. Once they start to lose focus, they start to make mistakes. Once they start to make mistakes, they end up losing. As I stated earlier, I have seen it happen. I have been a part of it. The LULL of our Spiritual Walk can be the same. Here is how it works. A kid gets saved. Early on they are on fire for the Lord. Over time, they start to lose that emotion. As they lose the fire and emotion, they start to lose focus. Maybe they stop going to church. Maybe they quit reading their Bible. As they start to lose focus, they become more prone to make bad decisions. As bad decisions increase they may eventually "lose" their faith. Have you ever seen that happen? Have you ever experienced that in your own life? Teaching and coaching baseball I have, unfortunately, seen this happen many times. I think Jesus hits on this topic in the book of

Revelations. In Revelations 2:4-5 Jesus says, "But I have this against you: you have abandoned the love (you had) at first. Remember then how far you have fallen; repent, and do the works you did at first. Otherwise, I will come to you and remove your lampstand from its place----unless you repent."

So we can experience a LULL in our walk with Christ and in our baseball games. In baseball, I coach pitchers so I am constantly in the dugout. There have been many times when I try to talk to guys and fire them up as they start to lose focus. I hope that between myself and the other coaches on our staff that maybe we have prevented some LULL's from happening during ballgames. The question is though: How do we prevent a LULL from happening in our walk with Christ?? I believe the book of Ephesians gives us many clues.

Ephesians was intended to be a circular letter that Paul wrote to the people of Ephesus, as well as others in that part of the world. The book gives clear instructions on how we can ensure that we are active and growing in our

Spiritual Walks.   To summarize:

1.   We are all chosen to live Holy and Blameless
     lives (Chapter 1)

2.   We are saved by Grace through Faith, and are
     then created for Good Works. (Chapter 2)

3.   God's Love and Power is beyond our
     imagination, but is available to believers
     (Chapter 3)

4.   God has equipped ALL of us with Spiritual Gifts
     and Blessings that He desires for us to use to
     Glorify and Honor Him. (Chapter 4)

5.   God calls us to be Imitators of Christ and to
     remove anything in our life that does not bring
     Him Glory and Honor (Chapter 5)

6.   God equips us to fight the Spiritual Battles of
     our lives.   (Chapter 6)

If we are to avoid the LULLs in our Spiritual Walk, then we
need to abide by Paul's instructions in the book of

Ephesians. For me, realizing God's Love and then His Power in my life was life changing. And then knowing that He has equipped me with the ability to Glorify His name and strengthen His body is amazing!! I have been chosen by God. We have all been chosen by God. WE can avoid these LULL's if we continue to pray that God will strengthen us with His power to use His gifts. There is something to be done every day for the Glory of God. There are no "innings" that are not important. 2 Corinthians 3:18 says "we are BEING transformed." It is not a one day process. God desires to work in us every day.

PRAYER:

God, I pray that through your love and power that I might avoid any LULL in my walk with you. I pray that I will continue to grow in the gifts that you have provided me so that each and every day I may be able to Glorify You and strengthen Your Body. I pray that you forgive me when life distracts me from the purpose that You have for me. Clothe me in Your armor so that nothing can keep me from running the race set before me. AMEN

LET'S PLAY: DISCUSSION OF

CHAPTER 6

1. Have you ever experienced a time in your life where you felt that no one understood or cared about you? Discuss

2. Are there other areas in our lives where we feel LULL'S? In other words are there times when we just don't feel connected to certain things?

3. Can you remember a time when you just felt that God was not there at all??

4. If you are a believer, do you experience times in your Walk when you feel God is very distant?

5. As a believer, what do those distant times feel like?
    What kind of thoughts go through head during
    those times?

6. Does God move or do we move?   Why do we
    experience distant times in our walks?

7. Read through the book of Ephesians.   What areas
    that were listed earlier do you feel you fall short in
    that has led to you experiencing LULL's in your walk
    with Christ?

CHAPTER 7: WINS (BLESSINGS)

I have been fortunate in my life to be part of a lot of successful teams. Winning baseball games is a great feeling. For some reason winning in baseball is better than other sports. I've played them all: football, baseball, and basketball. I think the feeling comes from the fact that baseball is so difficult. As I stated earlier, it's challenging physically, but more so mentally. It can even be extremely draining as a coach. There have been many games that I have walked away from feeling like I just took the SAT's (except I didn't fall asleep this time)

But, as mentally draining as the game can be, winning is exhilarating. In high school I was part of some successful teams. My freshman year we made it to the Elite 8 and had a legitimate shot to advance to the Final Four. My junior year was the best team I ever played on. Jody Pollock was our best player and led us to a Region Championship. He went on to start and succeed at Georgia Southern and then the University of Georgia, where I too was blessed to play. I like to tell people I watched a lot more than I actually played.   But, I did get to pitch some, and was part of some very successful teams.   In 2001, we won the SEC Championship and advanced to Omaha to participate in the College World Series.   I never pitched, and we went 0-2, but it was a great experience.

To be honest, I have experienced a lot more success coaching than I did playing.   Coaching just seemed to fit me.   The first time I had an opportunity to coach was working Christmas pitching camps with Coach Daron Shoenrock at UGA.   I was instantly attracted to it.   I knew going into my senior year at UGA that I would one day be a high school baseball coach.   Whatever doubt I had at the time went away when I got to pitch for Butch Thompson in 2002.   I had met Butch working one of the Christmas camps at GA and we began a good relationship that still exists today.   It was an honor to play for him my senior year.   He was not only a great pitching coach, but also had a passion for the Lord that I had rarely seen during my playing days.

I have now been coaching high school for eleven

years and during that time we have had a lot of success. In 2008 and 2012 we won State Championships. Winning a State Title is difficult. There are a lot of great coaches out there who have never won one. On top of the 2 State Titles, we have also won many Region Championships. At the writing of this book, I think we have won 4 in a row. Whether its winning titles or winning individual games, there is not anything better than winning in baseball.

Winning can eventually be something that is taken for granted. I think we have established that in Loganville now. We go into every year planning to win the Region and knowing that we have a legitimate shot at a State Title. Coaches, players, parents, and community have the same expectations every year. How quickly we forget that it wasn't many years ago when we were just hoping to be .500 at the end of the year. Winning will do that for you. It's like a form of dementia.

I used the term "blessed" earlier when I was talking about winning. The Bible uses the word blessed a lot. According to numerous sources that I researched the word

"Blessed" appears in the Bible more than 100 times. It seems that providing blessings are an important aspect of the Character of God. Throughout the Bible, God makes it clear that He desires to bless His people. Luke 11:28 says, "[28] He replied, "Blessed rather are those who hear the word of God and obey it.""

Many times when we think of blessings we think of good stuff. Lots of Christians struggle with the Blessings of God. I have to admit that if you look at it surface deep, it seems that God almost contradicts Himself. God says that He wants to bless us, but there are also many verses about the difficulties that we will have in this life. Are God's blessings based on our faith? Are God's blessings based on our work for Him? I have struggled with these questions a lot in my spiritual walk. When life seems to be going well, I start to think, "Man, God must be really happy with me." When life is difficult I start to think, "Man, God must be really upset with me." I will save you a lot of time and headache and encourage you to not walk the path I have. Life is tough!! There is no doubt about that, but our difficult circumstances have nothing to do with God's

Love or His desire to bless us!

God is good! 1 John 4:8 says, "Whoever does not love does not know God, because God is love." But the question is, what is love? My mom use to always tell me that I would never truly understand love until I had children. As a father of a 4 year old and a 17 month old, her belief has become true in my life. It's hard to explain. I always knew the love that my mom had for me, but kind of blew it off when she would talk about it, but make no mistake about it, there is something special about the way we feel about our children. I can't explain it. You can't either. But we have it. There is a special feeling when we look into the eyes of our children. There is a special hurt when we see our children in pain. There is a special joy when we see our children happy. If you have children, take that feeling that you have for them, multiply it by infinity, and you will begin to grasp the Love that God has for you.

The Bible says that God is Love. So, what does that mean? 1 Corinthians 13:7 says that "Love always

protects, always trusts, always hopes, always perseveres."
Other verses use the terms: bear, believe, hope, and
endure. Could we change that verse a little? God helps
us to bear all things! God helps us to believe all things!
God provides us the ability to hope in all things! God helps
us to endure all things! Man, that is special. Do you
always give your child everything that he or she wants?
No! At least I hope not. There are times when they have
to go through difficult times, right? Does that mean you
don't love them? NO!

Jesus truly discussed the concept of "blessings"
best in His Sermon on the Mount. The beginning of His
sermon is known as the Beatitudes. The term Beatitudes
derives from a Latin word meaning happy or fortunate. In
Matthew 5: 3-12 Jesus says:

3 "Blessed are the poor in spirit,

for theirs is the kingdom of heaven.

4 Blessed are those who mourn,

for they will be comforted.

5 Blessed are the meek,

for they will inherit the earth.

6 Blessed are those who hunger and thirst for righteousness,

   for they will be filled.

7 Blessed are the merciful,

   for they will be shown mercy.

8 Blessed are the pure in heart,

   for they will see God.

9 Blessed are the peacemakers,

   for they will be called children of God.

10 Blessed are those who are persecuted because of

righteousness,

   for theirs is the kingdom of heaven.

*11 "Blessed are you when people insult you, persecute you
and falsely say all   kinds of evil against you because of
me. 12 Rejoice and be glad, because great is your reward in
heaven, for in the same way they persecuted the prophets
who were before you.*

According to Jesus, "blessings" have nothing to do
with having an easy life. The true blessing in this life is
experiencing God. The true blessing is being able to be a
part of God. We don't love God because he has blessed us.

We love God because He first loved us. He loved us in spite of our imperfections and sin. He loved us "while we were still sinners" (Romans 5:8). I don't love my daughters because they are good. I love them in spite of their flaws. I love them even when they are bad. I loved them when they entered this world before I even really knew them. And I bet if you have children you can relate to me.

Blessings have nothing to do with getting stuff. We are not blessed because we have an easy life. To be honest, although miserable at the time, some of the most "blessed" moments in my life were at times when I just came through something difficult, when life threw a curveball at me, but somehow by the Grace of God, I adjusted and handled it well. I have heard so many hitters in baseball talk about the same thing. It's like they would love it if the pitcher just sat there and threw them fastballs belt high down the middle all the time. They would really be able to produce and the game would be easy, but I have noticed that guys really take pride in hitting that tough curveball. It's like they feel more accomplished. They didn't enjoy it when the pitch was thrown, but getting through it successfully has brought them excitement, more excitement than hitting that fastball.

Blessings are part of God's nature. Blessings are part of our nature. As I said earlier, I enjoy winning. I enjoy getting good stuff. I enjoy when life is on cruise control, but as a believer that is not what it is all about. Being a part of God's team is the greatest blessing we will ever experience. There is a deep seeded desire in all of us to have a connection with God. And the beauty of it is, GOD DESIRES US AS WELL. I can't explain it. It's not like He needs us, but God desires a relationship with us. The creator of the universe wants to "bless us" by allowing us to be a part of His Body.

Let's sit back and enjoy the ride of life. If we become a believer, will life be easy? NO!! There is no promise in the entire Bible that starting a relationship with the Lord will make things easy for us, but as stated earlier, God does tell us in His Word that He desires to bless us. We just have to understand what true blessings are. Our world and especially American society has greatly confused the concept of being blessed. God loves us. He desires the best for us, but sometimes the best for us is not having an easy life. We have to have faith. The Bible says in Hebrews 11: 1 "Now faith is the substance of things hoped for, the evidence of things not seen." We have to stick to the Word, which says that God wants to Bless Us and we have to have faith, regardless of life situations, that God cannot and will not lie.

PRAYER:

Thank you, God, for blessing my life. Thank you for allowing me to be a part of your team. Thank you for the good and the bad that life has offered me. I know that all things are working together for my good. Thank you for the truth of your Word that promises me your love and desire to bless my life. AMEN.

LET'S PLAY: DISCUSSION OF CHAPTER 7

1. Have you ever sat back and truly thanked God specifically for the blessings that you have been given? Why not.

2. List the top 3 Blessings that you feel God has provided for you.

3. How does God's opinion of Blessings differ from ours?

4. What if God took away one of your top 3 "Blessings"? Would your viewpoint of God be the same?

5. Do you write down when God answers prayers or provides you with blessings? Or do you only write down requests for God?

6. Why does God bless us in our life?

7. Does God bless us more based on our works or less because of our complacency?

CHAPTER 8:   9 PLAYERS

(SPIRITUAL GIFTS AND FRUITS)

This might be my favorite chapter!   Baseball allows for 9 players to be involved in the game at a time.   I guess if we got into the DH talk we could say 10, but there are only 9 guys on the field or 9 guys hitting at all times.   In baseball, 9 players will include a Catcher, Pitcher, First Base, Second Base, Third Base, Shortstop, Right, Left, and Center Field.

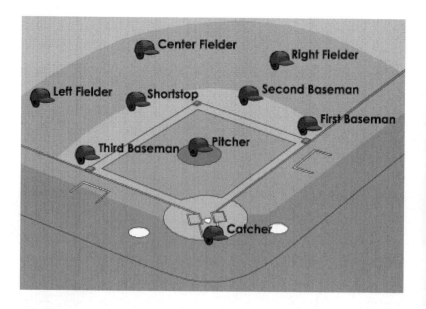

The picture above shows all 9 positions that are allowed on the field at one time. Is one position more important than others? NO. Is one position more difficult to play than others? Depends on who you ask. Is there anyone who is good at every position? Very rarely. I have seen guys that can pitch and do nothing else. I have seen guys who can really catch, but could never pitch. I have seen guys who can play center field, but can't field a ground ball at short stop to save their lives. You often times will hear coaches say that "pitching wins championships." I think that there is a lot of truth to that, but pitching "alone" will not win championships. I don't care how good your pitching is, if you can't "catch" it, you won't win. What's my point? Every position on the field is important. Are some positions more significant than others? Probably so. But, the stronger each position is, the stronger the team will be. There is a saying in sports and life that "you are only as strong as your weakest link." If there is a position on the field or an employee in a job that is weak, the entire team or work place will suffer because of it. I often times will tell my better pitchers that they should not be surprised if I am somewhat "hands off" with them.   Why?   Because I know it's important for me to develop the guys who are further down the rankings.   I know that if we are going to have a strong pitching staff, I must do a good job of getting the weaker guys better.   Too many times as coaches we invest too much into the "good ones." And forget, that our success comes from the strength of the team.

To me, there is an interesting similarity between the concept of 9 players on a team and the 9 Spiritual Gifts and Fruits that we are offered as believers.   WOW!!   I'm telling you, God has a heart for baseball.   HA!!   The Bible talks about both of these and it's important that we understand that there is a difference.   There are 9 Spiritual Gifts that as believers we have at our disposal.   There are also 9 Fruits of the Holy Spirit.   I believe that the 9 Fruits of the Spirit are more important than the Gifts themselves, but both are created by the Holy Spirit to equip us as Believer in Jesus Christ.   I once read that the 9 Fruits of the Spirit are like the "cake" while the 9 Spiritual Gifts are more like the "icing" on the cake.   Without the cake, the icing has no significance.   I personally like to eat the cake much more than the icing, but that's another conversation in itself (I got a bad sweet tooth). So what are these 9 Fruits and 9 Gifts of the Spirit?? The 9 Fruits of the Spirit are discussed in Galatians 5:22-23. Paul says, "[22] But the fruit of the Spirit is love, joy, peace, forbearance, kindness, goodness, faithfulness, [23] gentleness and self-control. Against such things there is no law. Against such things there is no law."

1. LOVE

2. JOY

3. PEACE

4. FORBEARANCE (PATIENCE)

5. KINDNESS

6. GOODNESS

7. FAITHFULNESS

8. GENTLENESS

9. SELF CONTROL

9 Fruits of the Spirit.   As we allow the Holy Spirit to work through our lives, these characteristics should begin to be shown.   You might look at this list and say, "No way!"   I would think that all of us would look at this list and feel overwhelmed.   If we were all honest, we could all pick out at least one of these that we struggle with.   Maybe it's PATIENCE, or SELF CONTROL, or maybe its PEACE.   The truth is that all of us as humans struggle with these.   I know I do.   I said earlier that I struggled with Anxiety. Yes, that's right.   I call myself a believer, but I struggle at times to live in PEACE.   Does that mean I'm not a believer? NO!!   It means that God is not done with me.   It means that I am "being transformed."   I didn't become a believer and God transformed me over night.   It is also important that we understand that it is only through the POWER of the Holy Spirit that we are able to live out these Fruits. Remember these are Fruits of the Spirit.   They are not ours.   The Holy Spirit has a "patent" on them.   Only He lives them out to the fullest .   Only He understands them. And only He helps us in the areas in which we are weak. Praise the Lord!!   It's interesting that Paul refers to these

as the "Fruit of the Spirit." Paul makes it clear that the Fruit is singular. It's not that we should be perfect with these Fruits if we call ourselves a believer, but instead it is the Spirit who has perfected Himself in these and will work them through us in times of need. We need more Patience, the Holy Spirit can provide! We need more Love, the Holy Spirit can provide!

Just as the Holy Spirit has 9 Spiritual Fruits that He desires to be displayed in our lives, so also there are 9 Spiritual Gifts. Now, let's make it clear that this is a topic that can be argued. Some people believe that there are less than 9 gifts, some people believe there are more. I don't think the number is important!! But, I think the focus should be on the gifts, the fact that our Loving Father desires to provide us with gifts. 1 Corinthians 12:7-11 says, "[7] Now to each one the manifestation of the Spirit is given for the common good. [8] To one there is given through the Spirit a message of wisdom, to another a message of knowledge by means of the same Spirit, [9] to another faith by the same Spirit, to another gifts of healing by that one Spirit, [10] to another miraculous powers, to another prophecy, to another distinguishing between spirits, to another speaking in different kinds of tongues,[a] and to still another the interpretation of tongues.[b] 11 All these are the work of one and the same Spirit, and he distributes them to each one, just as he determines." I love the end of this passage when Paul says that the Holy Spirit distributes as HE WILLS!! The above verse is not the only time that the Bible mentions Gifts of the Holy Spirit. According to my count, there are 23 verses that refer to "gifts" in the New Testament. As I stated earlier, many people will argue that there are more or less than 9 gifts. I actually really like some of the other references from the Bible on Spiritual Gifts. In Ephesians 4, Paul mentions the gift of teaching, the gift of evangelizing, the gift of shepherding, and the gift of apostles. All of these are Spiritual Gifts as well that cannot be ignored. And then in Romans 12, Paul talks about even more gifts like serving, leading, exhortation, and acts of mercy. So please do not get stuck on the 1 Corinthians and the number 9. I don't think it really matters!! The key is that the Holy Spirit provides us with Gifts. He provides all of US! Why? So that we can impact the Body of Christ. So that we can bring others closer to Christ. So that we can Glorify Christ through our lives. We spend so much time trying to develop our "worldly" gifts. I know I do!! I go to baseball coaching clinics. I go to coaching websites. I go to teaching workshops. I read books on teaching and coaching. Why? To develop my profession. I spend a lot of time to become a better teacher and coach. But, as a believer I must also be seeking opportunities to grow my Spiritual Gift. Unfortunately many of us do not grow our gifts. Many of us don't even know what our Spiritual Gifts are. I didn't for many years. I firmly believe that many Believers in Christ end up walking away from their faith because they don't feel they have a part in the Body. They don't feel they have a role. As humans, we all like to feel that we are important. Whatever we are doing, we want to feel needed.

So what do we do? First, we need to study the Word of God to discover what God says about Spiritual Gifts. For example, what are they? Second, we need to pray and seek wisdom for clarity on our specific Spiritual Gift. There are many websites that can help you discover your Spiritual Gift. I just recently had the opportunity to do this with my 9th Grade Boys Small Group at church. Most of those guys had no idea what their gift was. Shoot, most of them didn't know that there were Spiritual Gifts discussed in the Bible. Third, we need to seek ways that we can grow that gift. We should seek ways that the Holy Spirit can develop this gift in our lives.

In the Summer of 2013 I had the opportunity to go on a Mission Trip to Ghana, Africa. It was a 2 week Mission Trip that centered around us doing Pastor Conferences in the morning and Revivals/Youth Conferences in the evenings. It was the first mission trip that I had ever done over seas. I had never been to Africa before, so that in itself was extremely exciting for me. I am a Social Studies teacher, so I had taught on Africa many times and was always interested in going. The trip in itself would have been amazing! The country is beautiful. The people of Ghana are full of love and life. For the most part, we felt welcomed everywhere we went. I have never seen so many smiles over a two week period. Men like Apoku, Vincent, Solomon, and Dr. Charles truly represented the people of Ghana. They were men of God that had a desire to see the Body of Christ strengthened and the Love of God spread. The Spirit of the Lord is truly in the country of Ghana. I was blessed to be a part of the Mission Trip that got to experience that beautiful country.

From a teaching standpoint, one of the main topics that we focused on during the trip was Gifts. We did a lot of our teaching from the book of Ephesians. As I stated earlier, in Chapter 4 of that book Paul gifts such as teaching, pastoring, and evangelizing. The discussion of that book and specifically that chapter brought us into many conversations on "gifts" in general. There is a strong foundation in Ghana from the Pentecostal Church. Many of the churches that we went to, even if they were Baptist or Nondenominational, they would still feature many aspects of the Pentecostal foundation. Most of the church leadership and congregations put a huge emphasis on certain Spiritual Gifts. For the most part the speaking of Tongues, the gift of Healing and the gift to Prophecy were all extremely significant. Now please understand that I am not saying anything negative about these churches. I only desire to use this as an example in a discussion of Spiritual Gifts. On the flip side of this coin there are many American Churches that never even mention Spiritual Gifts. You bring up the Holy Spirit and Gifts in some of the American Methodists or Baptists churches and you might be forced to leave. I grew up in a Methodist church. The speaking of tongues was not even discussed. Who's right? Neither. We must be diligent that we allow the Holy Spirit to distribute gifts as HE PLEASES!! Spiritual Gifts should not be manmade, but they should not be ignored either! As the Word of God says in 1 Peter, we have "each" been given a gift, and that gift should be used to benefit others. I encourage you to seek the Spiritual Gift that God has given you. Seek it, allow the Holy Spirit to produce it in your life, and then use it to bless others and Glorify God.

9 Players, 9 Fruits of the Spirit, and 9 Spiritual Gifts from the Holy Spirit. WOW!! If we want a successful team in baseball, we need to have 9 players that are each doing their job. They are each using their specific talents to help the team achieve. It takes all 9!! In our Spiritual lives, we need to discover the power that we have through the Holy

Spirit. We have been provided with the Fruits of the Spirit.

The Holy Spirit Himself is the only one who has perfected

these characteristics. He desires to share them with us so

that we can continue to be transformed into the image of

Christ Jesus. Not only are we provided with this "Fruit",

but we also are blessed to be given Spiritual Gifts. These

gifts allow us to be active in the Body of Christ. They allow

us to hopefully bring others into the presence of Christ.

And finally through using the Gifts of the Spirit, we can

Glorify God with our lives. 9!! Whether its baseball or

spirituality, the number 9 is significant!!

PRAYER: Father God, I thank you for the Holy Spirit. I

pray that as a believer you might equip me with the Fruit

and Spiritual Gifts that only you can perfect in my life.

May I be open to how you desire to use me in the Body of

Christ. Forgive me for all the times I seek to improve my

worldly gifts and ignore my Spiritual gifts. May the Holy

Spirit do a mighty work in me so that I can bring Glory to

you. AMEN.

LET'S PLAY: DISCUSSION OF

CHAPTER 8

1. List the Fruit of the Spirit.

2. What characteristics of the Fruit of the Spirit do you feel you are sufficient in?

3. What characteristics of the Fruit of the Spirit are you lacking in?

4. Do you know your Spiritual Gift/Gifts?

5. Why is it important for us to know and utilize our Spiritual Gifts?

6. Use one of the following websites to research your Spiritual Gifts. Even if you know yours try it

anyway.

www.christianet.com/bible/spiritualgiftstest.htm

http://www.spiritualgiftstest.com/tests

http://www.ministrymatters.com/spiritualgifts/

7. Why is it important for us to grow in our relationship with the Holy Spirit?

CHAPTER 9: GEAR AND UNIFORMS (SPIRITUAL WARFARE)

As coaches meet at home plate before ballgames the umpires always ask: "Are your players properly equipped?" The answer is always yes. Equipment and uniforms are just as important in baseball as they are in any sport. Lots of times we look at football and think that it is by far the most dangerous sport for any kid to play. That thinking is probably right, but baseball is a close second. Although not encouraged, there is contact in baseball, and of course the ball itself can cause huge injuries. I have seen some gruesome injuries during my time with baseball. Of course there are the falls, the broken arms, broken fingers, and broken legs, but I have unfortunately seen much worse. I have seen teeth completely knocked out. One of the scariest events I ever saw was back in the Summer of 2003. I remember it extremely well.

2003 was my first year coaching at the high school

level.   Coach Segars approached me and asked if I would

be interested in being the head coach of the Loganville

American Legion team.   Post 233!   After he convinced me

that he would be around to help out (which didn't

happen!!!), I said yes.   I still joke with Segars about that

today.   I remember it well.   "I will be your assistant."   "I

will coach them up and you just run everything."   "I will be

at the games to help out."   What was I thinking in buying

all of that?   Now, please understand that I am only joking

about this.   As I stated earlier I am very fortunate to coach

at Loganville High School.   Coach Jeff Segars has been

instrumental to me as a coach and as a man.   Hey, I was

single at the time with no kids.   What else did I have to do?

It turned out that Bran Mills came onto our coaching staff

that summer, and being a single guy himself, I persuaded

him to help me out.   It was great!   We had a good time

coaching those guys that summer.   Mills coached third

and ran the offense, while I handled the pitching and

managerial type stuff.   I will never forget that team.   We

had a good group of guys.   Some true roughnecks!   Guys

like Trip Burt, Brett Rowden, Michael Tabone, and Anthony

Weatherford. These guys could play. Most of them did

not go off and play at the next level, but could have. I still

wonder lots of times what happened to Brett Rowden. He

was one of the best centerfielders I have ever seen play. He

had all the "tools." While at UGA I saw a lot of good players

and he ranks right up there with them. As far as I know,

when we got done that summer, he went back to Oconee

County and helped his dad run the farm.

One of the best memories I had with that team was

taking them to an East Cobb tournament. For those of you

that don't know, East Cobb is the Mecca of high school

baseball in Georgia. East Cobb and Perfect Game run a lot

of big time tournaments, and there are good players from all

over the country that come in to play. There is, however, a

little bit of arrogance from the East Cobb community.

Many of the kids who play East Cobb feel they have some

special place in the game that outsiders do not. So in the

summer of 03 we took that Post 233 team up to Cobb

County. Now, I'm sure you've already predicted what

happened. We waxed about every team we played. There

was a shock and awe on the faces of some of those travel

teams as they watched a Legion team play so well.

Now going back to the injury that I was discussing earlier. That same summer we were down in Albany playing in the State Tournament. We had a kid on the mound name Trip Mealor. He was 6'6" and about 24o pounds. He pitched in the low 90's. The game was going along pretty well and "Meat" as we called him was mowing down hitters. Then came the injury. A kid was hitting and Mealor threw a fastball that hit him square in the helmet. The hitter immediately dropped to the ground. Now I have seen that happen many times, but what I witnessed next scared me. The kid started going into a seizure. He was twitching and shaking and eventually even started throwing up. The ambulance had to pull out on the field to pick him up and take him to the hospital. It was scary!! Now, just imagine if he was not properly equipped. What if he had not had a helmet on? I think it's safe to say that he might have died. You see it all the time in the major leagues. Hitters are hit with a pitch or pitchers are lined drived with a hit. There are times when these players never play again. Some have even died from

125

the injury. I was shocked to learn a couple of years ago that High School baseball uses the AED more than any other sport. For those that don't know, the AED is a used to restart a heart once it has stopped or is not beating properly. That blew my mind!! So when umpires ask: "Are your players properly equipped." You better make sure your yes is really a yes. Before every game umpires will check helmets. They are probably the most important piece of equipment. If there are cracks or problems with the helmets the umpire will throw them out. I remember one high school game at Cedar Shoals when the umpires threw all of our helmets out because of cracks.

Baseball equipment and uniforms. Through all of these years of baseball the uniforms and equipment have basically stayed the same. Sure they have improved, but for the most part our players are dressed just like baseball players were 50-60 years ago. Pretty cool! Even when properly equipped, injuries can still happen. But, we hope that by doing it right we can prevent players from getting seriously hurt.

So what in the world does equipment and uniforms have to do with our Spiritual walk? Well, actually a lot!! The Word of God says that we should "put on the full armor of God." For us as believers, the armor of God is our equipment. It is our uniform. As a young believer I never understood the importance of this. I remember Mrs. Q asking me about four years ago: "Do you cover yourself and your family with the Armor of God in the mornings?" Of course my answer was NO! I didn't even really know what the Armor of God was. And I definitely didn't know why I needed to do it. In Ephesians 6: 10-17, Paul talks about the armor of God. He tells us why we need it. He tells us specifically what it is and how it will help us in our walk.

Before I get into what the Armor of God is, let's take a look at why we need it. The Bible says that as a Believer we have an enemy. Paul says in verses 11-13 "[11] Put on the full armor of God, so that you can take your stand against the devil's schemes. [12] For our struggle is not against flesh and blood, but against the rulers, against the authorities, against the powers of this dark world and against the spiritual forces of evil in the heavenly realms.

127

[13] Therefore put on the full armor of God, so that when the day of evil comes, you may be able to stand your ground, and after you have done everything, to stand." Whew! That is a mouthful. Lots of info here. Let's break it down. First, Paul says that we need the armor of God because we are fighting an enemy. Makes sense right? Baseball players get properly equipped to defeat their opponent. As believers we must do the same. But who is our enemy? Paul says here that our enemy is not of this world. It's not the people we get into arguments with. It's not our wife or children when we become angry. It's not that person that talks bad about us. No, Paul says that our enemy is the Devil. He says that our enemy is Darkness and Evil. If we acknowledge that God and Jesus are real and not just something that we have made up, then we must also acknowledge that Satan is real. As a young believer I never gave one thought to Satan. But as I have grown in my walk, I now realize that Satan is real and desires to do everything possible to destroy me. The Bible says that "Satan comes to steal, kill, and destroy." He desires to destroy our lives, our happiness, our marriages, our

families, and our careers. And the truth is he is good at it. Think of the most evil person you have ever heard of. Maybe its Hitler, Stalin, Mao, or someone else. Doesn't really matter. None of them can hold a candle to Satan. Just as everything about God is good, everything about Satan is evil. Should he scare us? No!! Why not? Because we have the Power of God. But, we have to utilize it.

So let's go back to the equipment. At the time the New Testament was written, the Roman army was the most powerful in the world. The Roman army had the best soldiers, weapons, and armor. So it's not a surprise that Paul uses this analogy to discuss how as believers we should put on our armor. So here is what Paul says we should put on, and by putting it on, how it helps us fight Satan:

1. Belt of Truth: (God is Truth. If we are NOT speaking, teaching, and worshipping in truth, we will be revealed. No soldier wants to go into battle without a belt and run the risk of losing his pants.)

2.   Breastplate of Righteousness: (It's not surprising that the breastplate protects our heart. Righteous living comes from the heart.   We will be tempted and persuaded to fall into sin if our heart is not in line with Jesus.)

3.   Sandals of the Gospel of Peace: (We are called as a Believers to spread the Gospel to others.   If we don't put on the Gospel first in our life, we are more likely to step into traps and injure our feet, making us useless for the Body of Christ.)

4.   Shield of Faith: (It is our faith that protects us. Paul says that Satan is constantly throwing arrows at us, and we must be sound in our faith in order to extinguish those attacks.)

5. Helmet of Salvation: (Our helmet is hugely important.   The Helmet of Salvation is our hope.   There might be times when we get discouraged or frustrated and want to quit, but we have to keep putting that helmet on. It is our hope.)

6. Sword of the Spirit: (The Word of God. Paul equips us with a shield, helmet, sandals, belt, and breastplate. All of those pieces of equipment are for defense. The one offensive weapon we have is our sword. And the sword is the Bible. Paul says that we fight Satan with the Word of God.)

So my question is the same for you that I was asked years ago. Do you cover yourself and your family with the armor of God? If you say no, I urge you to begin. It's never too late. Satan is real. We must believe that. Undermining him and his power only provides fuel to his fire. We would never allow one of our hitters to step into the batter's box without a helmet and bat. When they get into that batter's box, they are going into battle. In a similar way, when we wake up in the morning and prepare to go into the world we need to equip ourselves. The Bible says that Satan prowls around like a lion looking for someone to devour. Don't let that someone be you. I don't say this jokingly!! James 4:7 says, "Submit yourselves to God, resist the devil and he will flee from you." Jesus fought Satan with the word of God. We have that

131

same power. Wake up in the morning. Cover yourself and your family with the Armor of God. Study the Word, and allow it to be your sword to fight against Satan and his tactics. We can and will win!!

PRAYER:

Father God, cover me and my family right now in your armor. Protect us from Satan. Allow your Word to penetrate me so that I can fight against Satan's schemes. Thank you that through you I have power over Darkness. AMEN

LET'S PLAY: DISCUSSION OF CHAPTER 9

1. List the Spiritual Armor that the Bible says we have at our disposal.

2. What piece of Armor do you believe is the most significant? Why?

3. Why do you believe that "the sword" is listed as the Word of God? What does that say about the Bible?

4. What are some practical ways that you can use the Word of God to fight?

5. Why is it important for us to clothe ourselves in

God's Spiritual Armor?

6. As a believer, should I fear Satan?   Why or Why

    Not.

7. What does it mean when the Bible says that our

    battles are not against "flesh and blood?"   Explain

CHAPTER 10:   A ROUND OF

INFIELD/OUTFIELD (GETTING

PREPARED FOR THE GAME)

I can still remember as a player how much I used to love taking something called Infield/Outfield before high school games.   For those of you that don't know, Infield/Outfield is when defensive players go out before a game and work out at their position.   It normally works where a coach will take a fungo bat and hit 2-3 balls to each guy and then they make a play like they would in a game. It is a great preparation for the game.   It simulates situations and plays that might happen during the game itself.   Players are also given the opportunity to get their arms and legs loose.   Infield/Outfield can be particularly important when playing on the road.   In high school baseball there are lots of fields that are tough to play on. Although it has changed a lot from when I played in the late 90's, there are still lots of high school fields that need a lot of work.   The field I now coach at in Loganville is extremely nice for high school.   We put lots of time and effort into it. Coach Ryan is our "field guy."   He does an excellent job keeping it cut and maintained during the season.   Most teams that come to our field have positive comments about our park. But even at our field, Infield/Outfield is important for opposing teams. Sports experts don't talk about home field advantage for no reason.

I can remember back in 2008 a situation that occurred that explains just how important Infield/Outfield is. We were playing in the Second Round of the State Playoffs. We won the First Round in 3 games against a good Saint Pius team. They were really scrappy, and to be honest, we were not a great team, just lots of competitors and a really good Sophomore class that played well above their age. What we did have in 2008 was pitching. We always liked our chances in a 3rd game (baseball playoffs in Georgia are best 2 out of 3). In the Second Round we had to travel up to Rome High School. It was a good 2 ½ hour bus drive from Loganville. 2 ½ hours is a long time on an old yellow hound school bus. Those seats are not the most comfortable in the world. As a coaching staff, we knew that it was important to get our players there early and have time to stretch out and loosen up before we had to play. The first day we get there we end up splitting with Rome.

They had a really good #1 pitcher that ended up beating us 2-1 in the first game. We won the Second game behind a good pitching performance by a kid named Ben Marshall. He was a Senior on that team and would go on to pitch at Georgia State. So, what in the world does this have to do with taking a Round of Infield/Outfield?? Well, we ended up getting rained out the next day so our 3rd game got pushed back a day. You never want that in the playoffs. It can really mess up your pitching for the next round. We show up to Rome on that second day and get off that bus again extremely tight after that 2 ½ hour drive. As we are getting out on the field and getting our players ready to go, the Head Coach from Rome tells us that we can't take Infield/Outfield. He tells us that the field is too wet and he has worked all day to get it ready. Now, we all understood his point, but on the flip side of it we felt it was very important for our guys to take a Round. We felt it was important to get our guys out there after that long bus ride. We felt it was important to get our guys out there and see how the footing was or how the ball was bouncing with the wet surface. It turned into a confrontation between Coach

137

Segars and the Rome Coach. Long story short, we do end up taking a Round. And we end up winning that Series. And we end up winning the next 3 rounds and were crowned State Champions!! Infield/Outfield is important!

How does it work? Normally you have 2-3 guys at each position. The coach will usually hit the ball to the outfielders first going from left to right. Each outfielder will get the opportunity to throw 1-2 balls to 2nd, 3rd, and Home. After the Outfield gets their work in, the Infield goes next. Now remember, they have already been involved by catching and throwing balls around that came in from the outfield. The infielders will do the same as outfielders by getting ground balls and throwing it around. They throw to first, turn double plays, and field slow rollers. When it's all said and done, players have gotten a chance to move around and throw in preparation of the game. Infield/Outfield gets us ready to play the game!! It gets us ready to take on our opponent!! As a coaching staff we try to take advantage of Infield/Outfield to check out other teams. It gives us an opportunity to see the arm strength and athleticism of our opponents. 3rd base coaches that have to make decisions of when to send or hold runners up, watching an opposing team take a round can be crucial.

I have to tell one story that I remember from high school about taking a round. My high school coach was Tommy Knight. Coach Knight was a great coach who was also a man of God. I can still remember him picking me up on Wednesday nights to take me to Faith Baptist Church. For a young man that didn't always have a father around, that was crucial for me in my life. But Coach Knight was also very serious. He was intimidating to me. I didn't want to get on his bad side. One day at practice we were going to take a round of infield/outfield and Coach Knight decided to let us do Phantom infield. Phantom is exactly what it sounds like. You go out there and take a round but you do it with a phantom ball. The coach will act like he is hitting it. Players will act like they are fielding it and then throwing it. I never really like doing it cause I was a player that always liked to throw, just one of the things that I enjoyed in the game. But anyway we were doing it and our 3rd baseman who was also our #1 pitcher acted like he fielded a ball and threw to 1st. After making the phantom throw, he immediately dropped to the ground. He started grabbing his throwing arm and screaming out in pain. I remember Coach Knight running over to him. I can only imagine what was going through his mind. Losing your 3rd baseman is one thing, but losing your #1 pitcher is completely devastating. Luckily, the 3rd baseman was just joking. I would have never of thought to do that. I would have been scared of Coach Knight running me or maybe putting me on the bench. But he did it, and it was funny! But I don't think we ever did Phantom Infield/Outfield again. As a coach now, I don't blame Coach Knight.

As we prepare for a baseball game by taking a round, we must also prepare ourselves Spiritually for the game of life. I have learned over the years that in order to be all that God has called us to be every day, we must prepare ourselves. Just like we didn't just show up at Rome High school back in 2008 and begin to play the game, we should not go into a day without preparation. But too many of us as believers do that. We go throughout the day trying to defeat an opponent that desires to destroy us every day. So what should our "Spiritual Round of

Infield/Outfield" look like?

    1. Go to the Lord in the morning! I firmly believe that we should go before the Lord first thing in the morning. Before we go to work or school or whatever, we should spend some time with God. The Bible is pretty clear on this subject. I love the passage in Mark 1:35 that says "[35] Very early in the morning, while it was still dark, Jesus got up, left the house and went off to a solitary place, where he prayed." What a powerful reminder of how important it is to get up in the morning and go to God. There are so many other verses where we see God working "in the morning." We don't find the same number of verses about the afternoon or evenings. That's not to say that God is not available or at work throughout the day, but there seems to be something sacred about the morning. Is it easy to go to the Lord first thing in the morning? NO! I am so guilty of waking up in the morning and beginning an immediate checklist of the day. I am especially guilty of this during baseball season. My mind goes straight to practice plans or game strategies. I don't have a problem admitting this. I am human. I would be lying if I said

differently. But I do pray that God continues to

"transform" me in this area.   I can tell you from experience

that there is something special about rising before the sun

is out and spending time reading God's Word and praying!

If Jesus found that going to God early in the morning, was

important?   I would be an idiot to think otherwise.   I think

many times the problem that we have that makes it so

difficult for us is because we view this time as just one more

thing.   We fail to remember that we are spending time with

the creator of the universe.   The Alpha and Omega.   The

Beginning and the End.   It is a privilege that we can go to

God.   It's not just one more thing that we are have to do.   I

have to continue to remind myself of that!!

2.   Read the Word of God: 2 Timothy 3:16 says

that "[16] All Scripture is God-breathed and is useful for

teaching, rebuking, correcting and training in

righteousness, [17] so that the servant of God[a] may be

thoroughly equipped for every good work."   I believe that

this verse sums it up.   I love the part that says the Bible

and Scripture is "breathed out."   WOW!   Every verse in

the Bible is literally the breath of God.   Although men

wrote the Scriptures, they were led and inspired by God. There is nothing in the Bible that God did not want in there. People will argue that there were "books" and passages that were left out. I completely disagree with that argument. I have to believe and trust that anything that is not in the Bible today was not supposed to be in there. I don't care who put it together. It was still part of God's Will. Go back to I Timothy 3:16. Not only is scripture the Breath of God, but the verse says that it is also for TEACHING. We are taught the heart of God. We are taught the desires of God. We are taught the history of God. We are taught the plans of God. Unfortunately, in today's society there is a lot of manmade teaching. There is a lot of false teaching. We have to study the Bible to know the Truth. The verse goes on to say that scripture is for REPROOF and CORRECTION. What is reproof? Reproof is the act of being criticized or rebuked. The verse is saying that the Bible is perfectly adequate to show us where we are going wrong. If you study the words of Jesus and what he said about sin, I don't think you will feel very good. Jesus says that a married man should not even look upon another woman with lustful thoughts. He says that it's the same as adultery. He goes on to say that looking upon another with hateful thoughts is the same as committing murder. I can honestly say that I am guilty of both. The truth is that God's standards far exceed ours. Jesus did not come to uphold the law but to exceed the law. When I read the Bible, it is clear to me that I fall very short of what God desires. So the Bible is adequate at Reproof. But thankfully, the verse also says that the Bible is adequate for CORRECTING. We don't just read the Bible and walk away feeling guilty and condemned. Romans 8:1 says that "There is no condemnation for those who are in Christ Jesus." We can be encouraged that the Bible will rebuke us but will also correct us. God gives us a game plan. As a parent, I cannot constantly walk around and tell my daughters how bad they are. They will never improve their behavior unless I rebuke them and then correct them. When I get onto my daughter my goal is not to ridicule her and make her feel bad. Ultimately my goal is the same goal that God has for us. I know that when she starts to make better decisions, her life will be much more enjoyable. God knows the same about us! I get onto her, I rebuke her, but in the end I hope that I can help her to correct her bad behavior. Remember the Bible says that "God is Love." We can read the Bible and feel bad, but that is not the Lord's desire. Finally, the verse says that the Word of God is profitable for training us in Righteousness. So many people get confused on what God desires for us in our life. Nowhere in the Bible does God say that once we become Christians that we should be perfect. One of my favorite verses in the Bible says that we should "pursue Righteousness." When you pursue, you chase. It doesn't say that we should catch Righteousness, but that we should pursue it. We should run after it. The Bible provides the pathway or route for us to pursue that. It is my job as a father to do the same for my children. I teach, I rebuke, I correct, I provide a good path for them to pursue.

Now that we know what the Bible does for us, I think it is clear that we need to be in it daily. As I stated earlier, we need to meet the Lord in the morning, and I have found that one way we need to do that is by reading His Word. Some people like to read devotionals, others like to just open the Bible and read.   I think it is individual!   I am a

Devotional reader.   I am currently reading a devotional

called "Experiencing God" by Henry Blackaby.   I love it.

Every day it takes a piece of scripture and discusses it.

But it doesn't just explain the scripture; instead, it

discusses how I can apply it to my life.   We have to do that.

God desires for us to apply the Word.   The Bible says that

the Word of God is "alive."   It says that it is "active."   It

says that it is "sharper than any two edged sword."   This is

not a history book!!   I have heard it described as a Love

Letter.   I have had it described as an Instructional Manual.

I think it is both!   Is it difficult to read the Bible every day?

Yes!   Will there be days when you don't want to do it?   Yes!

But, we need to be disciplined.   It is amazing to me that I

have been reading the Bible pretty much for 20 years now,

and I still come across verses and stories that I haven't

experienced or verses that didn't speak to me in the past

will speak to me now because of different circumstances.

The Word of God is alive.   Let's get in it and read it every

day.

3.   Pray: As a young kid I was taught that every night

before I go to bed I need to pray. I was also taught that I

should always say a prayer or "blessing" before I eat. I

don't think there is any harm in any of that, but I now

believe that God desires much more of us when it comes to

prayer. There are many verses and many examples in the

Bible that refer to prayer. There are verses that discuss:

1. Why we pray

2. How we should pray

3. Where to pray

4. When to pray

5. Who to pray for

If quantity is an indicator of importance, then it is clear that

God believes in the power of prayer. Prayer is our ability to

communicate with God. The Bible does not say there is a

limit to prayer, but instead we have the opportunity to

spend time in prayer all throughout the day. It is our

chance to talk and listen to God. There are many

conversations that we could have on prayer. I will leave

that for a later conversation, and just for now stress that you study what God's Word says about prayer and then make it a daily routine in your life.

In baseball we have the opportunity to take Infield/Outfield before the game. It gives us the opportunity to get ready to "play." And just as that pregame time is important in baseball, we should do the same for our Spiritual Walk. In order for us to play the game of life as we are called by God, we need to daily take a good round of Infield/Outfield. We need to go to the Lord in the morning, spend time in God's Word and go to the Lord in prayer. In baseball and in our Spiritual Walk, preparation is the key to success. We should be as adamant about our daily time with God as Coach Segars was about our Infield/Outfield before the Rome game in the 2008 playoffs. That time with God is precious, and we won't play the "game" as well if we don't take advantage of it!!

PRAYER: Thank You God for your desire to have a relationship with us. Thank you for giving us your Word and allowing us to have insight into you through your Word. I pray that you move our hearts to go to you every morning. May you prepare us to fight each and every day. AMEN

LET'S PLAY: DISCUSSION OF

CHAPTER 10

1. List the different ways that we should be preparing ourselves daily to play the game of life.

2. Are you preparing yourself spiritually every day to tackle the game of life? If no, why not?

3. What areas of preparation do you fall short in? Meeting the Lord in the morning, reading the Word, or spending time in prayer.

4. What reasons do you have as to why you fall short in some areas of preparation?

5. What are some practical ways to improve those areas that we struggle in?

6. Can you think of someone that you know is good at

   preparing every day?

7. What are devotionals?   How can they help to get us

   into the Word more?

THE CLOSER (CONCLUSION)

I was fortunate to be a part of a pitching staff in college that had a very successful closer named Jeffery Carswell. Jeff transferred into UGA from Middle Georgia. Middle Georgia is a Junior College in beautiful Cochran, GA. They have had a great tradition of producing great baseball teams. There has been multiple guys play in the Major Leagues who came through that school. Jeff pretty much became the late inning guy for our team once he stepped foot on campus. The crazy thing about Carswell was he didn't necessarily fit the mold for a "slam the door shut" kind of guy. He was not very big and didn't throw very hard. But, Jeff had a couple of things really working to his advantage. First, Jeff had a really good breaking ball. He had one of the best curveballs I have ever seen. Second, and probably most important, Jeff had composure. He was able to keep his cool regardless of the situations he was put in. I truly believe his mindset was what set him apart!!

Most successful teams have a guy who can finish

ballgames. In baseball, we refer to these pitchers as closers. I am 34 years old, and have been fortunate in my lifetime to witness some of the greatest closers in the history of baseball. Guys like Mariano Rivera, Trevor Hoffman, and Billy Wagner. Great closers, at any level, are rare. I only saw a handful of really good ones at the college level and have seen even less while coaching high school. Most times in high school, if a pitcher has any talent, he will be a starter. At Loganville, we made a decision years ago to do everything possible to be good at the end of games. It can sometimes be a hard "sell" to high school kids. They grow up starting on the mound in games and most are not excited to pitch an inning here or an inning there at the end of games. But, I can tell you that the two state titles we won had guys who could finish a game. In 2008, we had Casey Shiver. Casey had every physical tool that you would want in a pitcher. He was tall, loose, and athletic. Casey had a really good arm and featured the best curveball I have ever seen at the high school level. He pitched for a number of years in the Texas Rangers organization. The 2012 team had a kid named Brandon Pergantis. Brandon

153

was very similar to Casey. Instead of a curveball, he had a sharp slider. Both guys could run it up into the low 90's at times, but mostly pitched in the upper 80's. Although we had a lot of good players and pitchers on both teams, I'm not sure we win either state title without these closers.

What makes a closer great?? I don't think there is one answer here, because I have seen so many different types of guys be successful. There have been: big velocity guys, one pitch specialty guys, sidearm guys, and even strike throwers. Take the three closers I mentioned earlier as examples. Rivera has always been a one pitch guy who features a devastating cutter. Hoffman was a low velocity guy who threw strikes and had a nasty changeup. Wagner was a small, left handed closer that could throw 100 and lived off of his fastball. All 3 guys were different physically. But, all 3 were very successful at what they did. I think the greatest characteristic that great closers have is a great mindset. I don't know if you call it confidence or composure or what? But whatever it takes mentally for a guy to get three outs in a tight ballgame, they had it!

Just as a closer is called upon to finish a ballgame and give his team a chance to win, I have called upon this chapter to wrap up this book and bring all the concepts together.   First of all, writing this book has been a blessing to me.   I am glad that God laid it on my heart and has opened my eyes in so many ways.   There really was never a moment in writing that I felt overwhelmed and miserable. I can remember back to college having to write 10-15 page papers and struggling the entire way through.   However, there were times when I doubted if I could finish it.   I have so many other significant things in my life that I worried at times if this was a waste of time.   I worried that I was spending time writing this book when I could have been playing with my children or spending time with my wife. But, I had to trust God.   And I am still trusting God.   I trust that He has a plan for this book!!

After completing the book and seeking some advice from different people I decided to reorganize the chapters. From a baseball standpoint, I don't think it mattered one bit what order the chapters were in, but spiritually I believe it does.   I hope that this final order makes more sense.   I have designed much of it to guide a person from the beginning of a relationship with Christ to an eventual everyday walk with our Lord. I know that I would have benefited as a young believer from a guide such as this. My heart is for young believers to read this book and study it with others. I think it would be most beneficial if used in Small Groups, Bible Studies, Sunday School Classes, etc. I pray that more mature believers will see it as a resource to help Disciple young believers in their walks. After all, that is what Jesus has called us to do. As Jesus was leaving the earth, He told His followers to go and make Disciples. I believe that as a follower of Jesus I have a job to do and you have a job to do. I think back to all the people who have led me in my walk throughout my life. People like my grandmother, my mom, my high school and college coaches, my wife, Ray Lawrence, Mrs. Q, Pastor Ronnie, Wayne Naugle, and all my small group guys have been instrumental in developing my relationship with the Lord. I'm sure there are others I am forgetting. I thank God for each and every one of them. But, I firmly believe that I can't just stop there. The greatest thank you that I could ever offer them is to do for others what they have done for me!!   That is my goal with this book.   I hope it becomes just one more resource that can be used to help people grow into a deeper walk with God!!   God Bless.

Made in the USA
San Bernardino, CA
15 December 2014